Things I Couldn't Tell My Mother

Sue Johnston

Things I Couldn't Tell My Mother

A MEMOIR

EBURY
PRESS

3 5 7 9 10 8 6 4 2

First published in 2011 by Ebury Press, an imprint of Ebury Publishing
A Random House Group company

The Random House Group Limited Reg. No. 954009

Addresses for companies within the Random House Group can be found
at www.randomhouse.co.uk

A CIP catalogue record for this book is available from the British Library

Every effort has been made to trace and contact the copyright holders of
photographs featured in the book. If notified, the publisher will rectify
any errors or omissions in subsequent editions.

The Random House Group Limited supports the Forest Stewardship
Council (FSC®), the leading international forest certification organisation.
Our books carrying the FSC label are printed on FSC® certified paper.
FSC is the only forest certification scheme endorsed by the leading
environmental organisations, including Greenpeace. Our paper
procurement policy can be found at www.randomhouse.co.uk/environment

MIX
Paper from
responsible sources
FSC® C016897

Printed in Great Britain by Clays Ltd, St Ives plc

HB ISBN 9780091938895
Export-only TPB IBSN 9780091944827

To buy books by your favourite authors and register for offers visit
www.randomhouse.co.uk

To my mum and dad.
And my son Joel – who will never read it!
And Gemma – who will.

This book is a work of non-fiction based on the life, experiences and recollections of the author. The names of some people, places, dates and sequences, or the details of the events, have been changed to protect the privacy of others.

Things I Couldn't Tell My Mother

ENA SHARPLES ONCE famously said of her mother's death, 'She just sat up, broke wind and died.' My mother would have definitely considered herself to be a cut above the fictitious Mrs Sharples and her mother. But as she lay in her bed, in the home where she'd been living for the past year, she did make one last Herculean effort to sit up, reaching out to be helped. Then she sneezed, lay back in bed, and I felt the life leave her, like someone had flicked off a switch.

She was ninety-two. I was sixty-three. These were her final moments, but the preceding weeks and even months had been long and exhausting.

As I reflect now, nearly four years after her death, I miss her. This may seem unsurprising; of course I should miss my mother. But things were far from plain sailing between her and me; our relationship was often difficult and fraught.

*

My mother began to sharply decline when I was filming *Waking the Dead*. Any time that I wasn't filming I would be making my way up the M6 to be with her. Then I received a call early in September 2007 saying she had taken a turn for the worse and that I should get there as soon as I could.

When I arrived in Warrington my mother had rallied and was sitting up in bed, alert and ready for me. She looked me up and down in my on-screen make-up and asked scathingly, 'What have you come as? You look like a bus conductress.'

This used to be quite a common insult when I was younger, as bus conductresses were known to wear thick pan-stick make-up. That I'd arrived to see my mum for what I thought would be the last time, only to be greeted with this, really makes me smile now. It was so typical of her. I stayed with her for a while and then reluctantly returned to filming in London.

A few days later I had another call. The nurses said they were sure this time that this was it. On the way, I got a flat tyre but I didn't stop. I think that I knew this really was the last time I would be making the journey. Everything and nothing was going through my mind. I was very emotional – racked with anxiety and upset, tired yet wired.

When I arrived at the home my mother was lying in bed, looking tiny and frail. There was no caustic put down this time. She just looked helpless and fragile. She was awake and aware that I was there but quiet and restful, slipping in and out of consciousness. I took her hand and vowed to stay by her side. I would remain there for the next four days.

This time to be with my mother was a privilege that I know many people aren't afforded. And as fraught, surreal and sad as it was, I was mindful that I had the opportunity to say things to her that I might not have normally said. Over the years I have had more than one occasion to want to tell my mother exactly what I thought of her, and not all of it complimentary or pleasant. She had always been a difficult person to deal with – someone who, I'm sad to say, found it very difficult to show affection or warmth towards me. It seems strange to admit this and yet at the same time she was my mother and I still loved her. As close relationships in life often are, ours was complicated.

My mother was obsessed with the notion of people getting ideas above their station. Having a daughter who was educated and followed her own path in life definitely fit into this category. There were many times when I just wanted her to be proud of me, but it seemed she never was.

But in these, her final days, as she lay in bed and I sat in the chair next to her, I wouldn't go as far as to say that none of the things that made me angry about her didn't matter, but they certainly didn't need airing now. It seemed to me to be a time for peaceful acceptance. As she became more vulnerable I felt things soften between us. I suppose it was because she needed me and I was very happy to be needed and to help.

With all of this time to think, with nursing staff and relatives coming and going, but me as a constant in the room with my mother, I felt I needed to say something to her – for her to hear something from me that was from my heart. Something I could say with absolute honesty.

I took her hand and said, 'Mum, I had the best childhood I could ever have had.'

Tears sprang to her eyes. I held her hand, which was gnarled with arthritis but she had enough strength for me to feel that she was holding on to me. Things changed as I got older, but it was true I really did have the best childhood and I needed her to know that.

*

Since her death, I have realised that whatever age we are, we all feel like children at times, even when there may be no one there to be a child for. Only last week I found myself hovering near the phone: I had found a recipe that I knew my mother would have liked and I wanted to tell her about it. Grief seemed to hit me all over again when I knew I couldn't have that conversation. It was only a small thing but she would have been interested in my discovery and it made me very sad that I couldn't share it with her.

My aim with this book is to look back over my life and explore what it was I couldn't tell my mother, and why that was. But also – and more importantly perhaps – I want to set down a record of all the love and life, loss and laughs: all the big things, and the small things. Everything I wanted to tell my mother but felt I never could.

Chapter One

I WAS BORN IN my aunty Millie's house in Warrington during the Second World War. My mother Margaret was staying at Millie's while my dad was away with his regiment. It is fitting that I was born in the thick of my extended family because although I was an only child I always felt part of a large clan.

My mother and her sisters would take turns to stay at each other's houses. The reason they gave was 'to keep the houses aired'. It seemed that everything needed 'airing' in those days. 'No wonder you've got a cold,' my mother would say, 'that top's not even aired!' So the houses were occupied in rotation in order to keep them aired, but I'm sure the real reason was the reassurance of safety in numbers.

My father, Fred, was in the Royal Engineers and was stationed in Portsmouth. At around the same time that my mother found out she was pregnant with me, Dad came down with an illness. He was throwing up every morning and eventually they took him into the field hospital to have him checked over. They couldn't find anything wrong with him, but then he happened to mention that my mother was pregnant. The doctor told him he knew exactly what he was suffering from: psychological morning sickness. Apparently it was quite common! While my dad was hospitalised his unit flew to Syria, where they were targeted and many of his regiment killed. Dad always used to say, 'Our Sue saved me.' When I was younger this was just a story but thinking about it now, it must have been quite harrowing for Dad, knowing how close he had come to death and to have lost so many of his comrades.

My mother would tell another story of a time my father was preparing to go back to Portsmouth. He turned to wave goodbye to her through the window, not looking where he was going, and as he did he walloped his head on a lamppost. He staggered back into the house, a great gash oozing blood from his head. My mum and her sisters had no time to be sympathetic, they were too busy doubled over laughing. Poor Dad needed stitches and ended up having to stay off for another couple of days. So my dad could say that he was hospitalised twice during the war – once for morning sickness and once for walking into a lamppost!

I often think about those years when I was first in the world and what it must have been like for ordinary people living through this extraordinary time. They were living on the edge in a very real sense. No one knew how events would unfold; all that they could do was pull together and hope for a positive outcome. My aunty Millie would always say about the war, 'Well, we just had to get on with it,' and she was right, what choice did people have? It seems to me that the only stories that were ever told about the war were as jokes or broad brushstrokes, never detail. The horror of war simply wasn't mentioned, except with gallows humour. It was as if that entire generation had accepted their lot – whatever happened during the six years between 1939 to 1945 stayed in those years.

They were an extraordinary generation, they were never indulgent or self-pitying about what they'd had to face. It does make me think that we're so very nannied now. I don't know how people would survive if they had to face the same thing. When the war ended, everyone was, of course, thrilled, but I can't help thinking that after all that time living on their wits, the return to everyday life must have been a difficult adjustment, even if it meant they might get the chance to actually clap eyes on a banana!

During the war, Liverpool and Warrington were a target for the German bombers. Liverpool, because it was a port and hub for industry and Warrington because after Pearl Harbor, when the Americans entered the war, it became an American air base. The place was swarming with GIs and my mum and her sisters would talk later about getting stockings and chocolates from the American soldiers. They spoke very highly of them, saying they were extremely courteous and generous. They used to go to the dances, but as far as they were concerned it was all very innocent. Other women did have relationships with the GIs that landed in Warrington and there was the common saying that they were Overpaid, Oversexed and Over Here. But I think as far as my mother and her sisters were concerned they were just Over Here, and they were glad of the stockings.

I arrived in the world on 7 December 1943. At that time women were expected to stay 'in confinement', they had to rest up in bed for several days and get their strength back after giving birth. While Mum was lying there a few hours after having me, looking at her new baby and minding her own business, the air-raid sirens began to wail. My aunties Millie and Ena came charging in and took me out of my cot, wrapped in my blanket.

'Where are you going?' my mother asked.

'To the shelter, of course,' Millie said, swaddling me and holding me tight. Millie had an Anderson air-raid shelter in her back garden that she and her sisters were well acquainted with.

'She's a tiny baby, we can't leave her in the house,' Ena added, matter-of-factly.

'What about me?' my poor mother implored.

'You need to stay there. You're in confinement.'

And with that the sisters were out of the door with me bundled in their arms, while my mother had to lie there and hope that the bombs that were dropping all around paid due respect to the notion of confinement and left her alone.

So this was my rather unceremonious introduction to the world and I was named Susan. It wasn't the one my mother had intended for me. My mother wanted me to have her name. I was to be Margaret Jane after both her and her mother and my father was duly sent to register the birth. I'm not sure what happened between him leaving the house and getting to the registry office but with uncharacteristic bravery he decided that I should be called Susan. The name didn't have any family connection for either my mother or father, I think he just liked it.

So here I was, Susan Wright. Hearing my first name and my maiden name together always makes me smile. You were only ever addressed by your full name at registration time at school, or if you were in trouble. If someone shouted 'Susan Wright!' at me now I'd still drop everything and wonder what I'd done. My mother always referred to me as Susan, never Sue. She would shout me in for my tea when I was a little girl. 'Susan!' the cry would come down the street. I would, of course, always try to wring out another few twists of the skipping rope.

One of my first really vivid memories of my mother is of me playing in the street waiting for her to return from an afternoon in Warrington. She rounded the corner and I saw her and waved excitedly. She had had her hair cropped. In those days most women we knew seemed to have a regulation perm, or their hair was rolled back and pinned around their head, a severe look that made them look older than they were.

So to see my mum with her short hair made her seem so glamorous and I was really proud of her. She was wearing a suit, a skirt suit as Mum never wore trousers. In fact, the first pair of trousers I managed to convince her to buy was when she was in her eighties. She always said she'd feel underdressed wearing trousers.

Mum had dark well-shaped eyebrows, which I inherited from her. She had blue eyes and a lovely nose but I inherited my dad's! The cropped hair didn't last long and the perm soon crept back in but Mum always looked very smart.

My parents made a handsome couple. Dad was five foot ten and very trim; he had a bit of a swagger when he was younger. He was a great swimmer and his physique showed it. When I was a girl I found a certificate and asked my dad what it was. He bashfully told me that it was awarded to him because years before I was born he had saved a man who was drowning off Blackpool pier. The man had got into trouble and Mum piped up to tell me that Dad had jumped in with no thought for his own safety. I was proud to think that if it hadn't been for my dad, that man would probably have died.

Dad had huge blue eyes and fair hair. He began to lose it as he got older and although he never had a comb-over he did have a few persistent wisps of hair that he carefully maintained. My dad, like my mother, was always very well turned out. He wore a trilby hat and a shirt and tie. I once bought him a Liverpool club tie and he was as proud as punch to wear it. Dad worked as a plumber both before and after the war. Mum had worked before she married Dad, in the box works, a box-making factory. She started as a machinist but had a shocking accident, running an industrial-sized needle through her fingers. She carried the scar until the day she died. After the accident she was moved to the assembly line, where she worked alongside her sisters Millie and Ena.

The house where I grew up was ten miles away from my aunty Millie's in Warrington. It was on the outskirts of Liverpool in a place called Whiston in a newly built estate, owned not by the council but by a landlord. I remember that the rent collector would come every week; we never saw the actual landlord but he was talked about in reverential tones. He had money when everyone else was on their uppers.

The houses were all semi-detached except for the four in our row. It was as if they'd got to the last plot and thought, 'Come on, lads, we can squeeze four in here.' The house itself was plain-fronted, a cheap-as-chips build with a small front garden, but as my family lived on the corner plot we had a larger backyard, which gave me and my cousins room enough to play and for my father to tend to his beloved plants.

It wasn't just the rent collector who knocked on our door every week. The pop man would come on his horse and cart and we would hand back our bottles and get a discount on that week's cream soda or dandelion and burdock. The rag-and-bone man would pass by on his horse and cart shouting 'Any Old Iron' but we could never really make out what he was saying, to us he just sounded like a strangled donkey shouting 'Eeyore!' The coal man would come around, heaving his sacks of coal on his shoulder. It was so cold in those days, we would wake up with icicles on the inside of the windows. When I was ill my dad would come up and put some coal in the grate of the fire in my room. I still hanker after a fire in my room like the one I had as a child. The milkman was also on a horse and cart and again we would give him back our bottles in return for that day's milk. I'd like to say to my mum, 'See we were green back then, weren't we? Recycling and we didn't even know it!'

I never felt that we were going without because everyone was in the same situation. We did not expect to have anything more. It was before we had TV so there were no advertisements telling us what we should want next and even if there had been we didn't have any money to buy them. Sweets were rationed until I was at junior school and I remember clearly the first day the ration was lifted and we were all given pennies to go and buy some sherbet.

We didn't have many toys or things to play with, every family had the same board games – Ludo, Monopoly, Snakes & Ladders, and a pack of cards for the adults. My mother would dye her legs with gravy browning and draw a line up the back of her legs to make it look as if she was wearing stockings. I suppose it was a primitive version of fake tanning.

We had a bath once a week. Heating the water for a bath involved lighting the fire, so if the fire wasn't lit my mother would boil a pan of water and give me a wash with that.

One of these bath days was the day before Warrington Walking Day. The Walking Day is a yearly event that is still being held today, originally it had been organised by churches in the area. It was essentially a parade and there was a fair afterwards and we would receive a few pennies to go on the rides. Everyone in the area took part.

I was very much looking forward to the parade the next day. Mum took some boiling water in a pan, brought it into the bathroom and set it down at the side of the bath. I was faffing around with the plug. As she went to pick up the boiling water, I got in her way and she spilled it all over my foot. I immediately began screaming in pain, my mother panicked and whipped off my shoe and sock, taking the skin with it. I was in agony and absolutely hysterical. Uncle Joe, my friend Valerie's dad and our neighbour, was passing our house and heard the commotion. He came inside to see what was going on. Seeing me sitting on the mangle, where my mum had plonked me so she could get a better look at my foot, he looked terribly shocked.

'Ring an ambulance, Joe, please!' Mum pleaded.

Poor Joe only had one leg but he turned and hopped to the phone box as quick as that leg could carry him.

An ambulance arrived to take me to hospital. I was bandaged up and sent home, and a nurse came round to our house every day to give me an injection. For a couple of months I had to use a wheelchair to get about. It was very painful and quite traumatic. I missed the walk, of course, and was very sad to have to sit at home ailing while everyone else was enjoying themselves.

I was only little at the time but I could tell that my mother was horrified and blamed herself, even though she would say, 'Why were you messing about like that?' She was right, it was me messing about that had caused it, but she felt guilty because she was a mother and that's what mothers do! Poor Mum. I still have that scar on my foot. I have the ugliest feet in the world and getting a scar on one seems to me to be adding injury to insult.

We weren't Scousers, we were Woollybacks, as the real Liverpudlians used to call us. The term is derived from the time of the industrial revolution apparently, when people from Lancashire and Cheshire used to wear a form of sheepskin. But ask around at a Liverpool football match why they use the term 'Woollyback' and they'll give you a very different reason involving relations with sheep – charming! Even though I have always embraced everything Liverpool has to offer, I have always known I'm not, I'm sad to say, a dyed-in-the-wool Scouser.

*

I have so many memories of my childhood that trying to pinpoint the earliest isn't easy and it seems like such a long time ago! But certainly my fondest early memory is of sitting on my mother's knee. We were in the living room as *Listen with Mother* came on the radio. I remember it was on at five to two in the afternoon and I can hear the tinkling intro clearly and the feeling that accompanied it. *Here comes our story…* I would think.

I felt very encircled by my parents when I was younger, very loved. Mum would nip to the corner shop and say to me, 'Stand on the chair and watch out for me, I'll only be a minute.' So I would stand in the window, watching her as she walked to the end of the road, disappear momentarily and then reappear round the corner again. She wanted me to know she wasn't going far and that I was safe.

Although I was an only child I never felt that I was on my own. My dad's family lived nearby in Whiston and my mother's family were not far off in Warrington and we saw them all the time. My dad was one of six, but that seemed like a small family compared to my mother being part of a massive brood of twelve!

My cousins Pauline and Marjorie, Ena and Millie's daughters, were like sisters to me when I was younger.

Although, I have to say, we didn't all scrub up in quite the same way. Pauline and Marjorie were always well turned out. Everything was clean and pressed and remained so throughout the day. I started out in the same orderly fashion – my mother would always make sure of it – but as the day progressed I would attract muck of all description, always the first to get grubby and the last in the bath if I could help it. I was a total tomboy and this distressed my mother who, as someone who never stepped foot out of the house without looking immaculate, had obviously hoped for a more kempt daughter. I remember very clearly once being made to walk behind my mother because I had been playing in the mud and she evidently felt I was bringing shame on the family. I couldn't have been any more than three at the time. The fact of the matter was I was a grubby child. Any bit of dirt, I'd find it. My mother would find me rummaging under seats on the train, surfacing with old cigarette butts hanging out of my mouth. If a bird pooed you could guarantee that it would land on me, and no amount of saying it was lucky would convince my mother that it was fine to parade around with bird muck on your coat. It didn't bother me that I was thought of as the scruffy one, and I know that my cousins quite enjoyed being the neat ones too.

I think that my tomboy ways may have been a direct reaction to my mother's assertion that she had always wanted a boy. It was something that she would tell me quite often – 'You were meant to be a boy' – as if the fact that I'd popped out a girl was in some way my fault. She even had a name: Michael. There was also the odd comment that led me to believe I was a 'mistake' and that she had never intended to be a mother. I think the fact that she came from such a large family put her off having children. Also, this was during the war and it was such a time of uncertainty that I'm not sure the idea of bringing a child into the world was something she and my father even considered. But once she had me she must have realised that this was what she was 'meant' to do as she certainly took on the role of matriarch of the house with great gusto.

I don't mean to sound melodramatic when I say that comments like this made me feel that I was never quite wanted by my mother. It was just the way it was in our house. Of course, it was never addressed by us because in our family we just didn't talk about how we felt. I'm sure I wasn't supposed to take it to heart; it was something Mum said to try to get me to be better behaved. 'I'm just telling you for your own good,' was one of her mottos and she stuck by it. I could never have sat my mother down and said, 'So, Mum, you say that you wanted a boy instead of me – do you know how that makes me feel?' She would have shot me down with one of her vinegar looks and told me in no uncertain terms that if she had had a boy he wouldn't be trying to have conversations like this with her!

As a child I spent a lot of time at my grandparents' in Warrington. It was a large three-bedroom semi-detached that they rented. It had a big bay-fronted window and the house formed an L-shape around the backyard with the dining room, kitchen and back kitchen overlooking it. We always used the back door, never the front. In fact I'm not sure who would have been allowed through the front door as my grandmother wasn't much for visiting dignitaries. Everyone was treated the same, so I can't think who might have got their foot through it.

But as large as it was for a semi I could never quite work out how they had managed to fit twelve children and two adults in there when my mother had been growing up. I would go upstairs to the bedrooms and stand for hours trying to work out where they had all slept. Eventually I asked my mother how the logistics had worked and she replied as though it was obvious, 'The girls were in one bedroom, the boys in another, of course.'

My grandmother – my mother's mother – was a large lady and round, with ruddy cheeks and a face that reminded me of a toasted bun. Her hair was grey and pulled back into an untidy French pleat that had strands of grey hair straggling out from all sides as if fighting to escape her hair band. She was a real character who had a healthy disdain for cleaning and didn't care who frowned upon her for it, something I have to say I think I may have inherited.

She was very capable in other domestic areas though. A self-taught seamstress, she made everything from coats to wedding dresses for an array of customers who would come to the house. Her children acted as a team, the older ones looked after the babies when they came along, wiping, feeding and cleaning. They would pick up the odds and ends of material that lay discarded around the house and would try to keep on top of this industry that my grandmother had created.

My grandmother dressed her own daughters; all six of them immaculately tailored. She used to buy *Vogue* and copy the designs from there. And when us grandchildren came along she dressed us too. Pauline, Marjorie and I would all be dressed the same, I think we quite liked it – identical, until of course I got myself covered in dirt. All my grandma's daughters had an impeccable sense of style that they got from her. I also have a huge love of clothes that I attribute to the time I spent with my grandmother. Having handmade tailored clothes from an early age obviously made me sartorially savvy.

As well as sewing my grandma loved to cook and bake. Cooking is also a passion of mine; I love to cook for others but cannot lay claim to my grandmother's prolific abilities. Her house always smelled of apple pie or custard tarts, or mince on cottage pie days. We would arrive at the house to be greeted with piles of baking – lemon meringue pies stacked next to huge chocolate éclairs that oozed cream. My grandma was a powerhouse of a woman, and looking back I don't know how she managed to do everything she did. She just seemed to be able to do ten things at once, a skill learned, no doubt, from having to deal with all those kids! My mother and my aunty Millie used to say with great admiration, 'She was a marvellous woman, our mother.'

My mum's dad was the strong, silent type. As a small child I found him quite distant towards me, but I wanted to know him and when he did say something I used to sit up and listen, as it was always something well thought out and considered. When he did speak to me he had a knack of making me feel very special. A few years ago I was asked to go on the BBC programme *Who Do You Think You Are?* where you delve into your family history. I knew that my grandfather had been from a well-to-do family and had turned his back on his privately educated upbringing to pursue a life on the railways. But here I learned how his own father, my great-grandfather, had dragged himself up by the boot-straps from a life of poverty in Carlisle to being a hotel owner and a man of considerable means. When my grandfather got married, on the wedding certificate under 'Father of the Groom', my great-grandfather had written, 'A Gentleman' as his occupation. It's funny to think that this was my mother's grandfather. I'm sure, hotelier or not, thinking himself a gentleman yet having come from the Dickensian slums of Carlisle would certainly have provoked a few choice words from my mother – it must surely rank as 'getting ideas above his station'.

The fact that my grandfather then turned his back on this privileged life no doubt caused ructions within his family, but he went off to do a job that he loved. He always had the nickname 'The Duke'. Whether it was given to him affectionately because of his background or whether it was something that stuck because he was an engine driver and therefore top dog, I have no idea. Anyway, he wasn't just any train driver I was told as a child: he drove one of the most iconic steam engines in the world, the *Flying Scotsman*. Not so, the *Who Do You Think You Are?* programme informed me. He was indeed a steam engine driver but he only ever worked on the west coast and the *Flying Scotsman* went down the east coast. A childhood belief was shattered by this revelation. However, I did receive a kind letter from someone after the programme aired, telling me that I shouldn't lose heart. The *Flying Scotsman* had travelled down the west coast from time to time and may well have been driven by my grandfather. I do hope so – I built any popularity I had at primary school on this connection!

It doesn't matter, though, as one of my most magical moments in childhood was to do with my grandfather and his steam train – *Flying Scotsman* or no *Flying Scotsman*. My mother and I were standing on the platform at Eccleston Park station waiting to catch the train to Liverpool. A steam train soon approached and the train driver was hanging from his cab, whistling to my mother. 'Margaret!' he shouted. My mother gave him a disdainful look. Who was this uncouth man hollering at her at the train station?

'Take no notice, Susan,' she said, taking my shoulders and positioning me away from the train. As the engine came to a stop we both realised it was my grandfather. My mother quickly changed her tune.

'Hello!' she said, suddenly all smiles to her dad. 'I was wondering who was shouting at us. Come along, Susan.'

We boarded the train and took our seat. It was a compartment, enough to seat six people at the most, with two sets of bench seats facing one another. I sat down on one of the seats. I was only about five at the time so my legs dangled over the edge, half a foot from the floor. I ran my fingers over the heavy weave of the upholstery. There were three pictures of places that the train no doubt stopped at on the wall. The doors and trim were a dark walnut colour and over my head there was a mesh luggage holder. The carriage smelt musty but not old, just grand. I was so excited this was my grandad's train. No one else's grandad had a train that I knew. My mother and I sat in the compartment and admired our surroundings. I could have stayed there all week.

When we pulled into Liverpool my grandfather came and got us and brought me to the front of the train where he lifted me up into his cab. He then introduced me to his fireman, the man responsible for shovelling coal into the fire to keep the steam pumping. Grandad showed me all the dials and the wheel and explained what being an engine driver entailed. Of course it all went over my little head as I stood there agog. But I was utterly thrilled that my grandad was the driver of such a big steam train. That bought me a lot of brownie points at school!

One thing that I clearly remember about my grandmother and grandfather's house was the huge amount of crockery and silver they had, obviously a legacy from the hotel days when my grandfather was a boy. The amount of silver was mesmerising and I would always be returning to the cupboard for a peek, just to see that it was still there. It seemed so precious to my young eyes. There were large coffee pots and teapots, sugar bowls, cruets, cutlery and trays all with Globe Hotel – the hotel that my great-grandfather had owned – stamped on them. This seemed like such treasured possessions to me as a little girl. The idea that we had family silver!

My father's mother died just before I was born. She never knew my mother was pregnant with me. Everyone always said what a lovely woman she was and I often felt that I had missed out on meeting someone very special. My father's father lived around the corner from us in Eccleston Park with two of his children, my uncle Harry and aunty May. Just along the road from them lived Aunty Reenie, Uncle Alec and my cousin Alec. About a mile away was Uncle John, Aunty Ada and my cousin Lavinia, and around the corner from them was Uncle

Bert and his wife Lynne, and their daughters Catherine and Elizabeth. It sounds like we were all living on top of one another but it just felt normal. Everyone I knew had his or her families close by.

Aunty May was very much part of my life in Whiston. She was a midwife at Whiston Hospital and during the war had nursed injured soldiers. She would come to our house most weekends and she would always have two bags of sweets for me, never one. And as I'm writing this it's just occurred to me that I do exactly the same thing. I always buy two of everything, *just in case*. Just in case of what I'm not sure! But I would seek refuge at her house whenever I was in need of advice or felt that I was in trouble. She was a great listener and I felt that I could sit with her and air my problems.

Aunty May had never married but always wore a little diamond engagement ring. One day I was sitting with her watching TV. Aunty May was the first person in our family to get a television and it was big news when it arrived. Every Saturday I would go to her house and we would watch *Six-Five Special*, a forerunner of *Top of the Pops*. As we were sitting there I plucked up the courage to ask her where the ring had come from. She said that it was from a Belgian man that she had met in the war, he was an injured soldier convalescing over here and she was his nurse. When he recovered, he went back overseas with the intention that he would return and they would marry. But he was killed on his return to active service.

Aunty May was heartbroken and never married after that. I went to see Aunty May three days before she died, shortly after her ninetieth birthday, and she was still wearing that ring. It makes me sad to think that she lost the love of her life at such an early age and then carried a candle for him until her death. There was never any other man in her life.

I went to Whiston Infants. My infant school teacher's name was Miss Cross and we would say 'cross by name, cross by nature', making sure that she never overheard us as we didn't want to incur any further wrath than she was already more than happy to dish out. She even looked cross, with her jet-black hair and features that wouldn't have looked out of place on a crow.

I went happily to school on the first day but the next day I woke up and said to my mother, matter-of-factly, 'I don't think I'll go to school today, thank you.'

My mother, with a look that could curdle milk, said, 'There's no "think" about it. You're going to school, young lady!'

With that I was dressed and whisked out of the door, my feet barely touching the floor.

I wasn't having this, I decided. They might have got me there under false pretences for one day, but I wasn't going again. As all of the other children filed obligingly through the school gates, I clamped my hands around the railings and clung on for dear life. My mother tried to pull me off but I was having none of it. 'I'm not going in!' I protested. My poor mother. In the end she gave up trying to extricate me from the railing herself and marched into the school, asking the head teacher if she would be kind enough to come outside and prise me away from the school gates and into the school itself.

The head came out and looked at me. I glared back, my face puce with defiance. 'Come on now, Susan, let's have you inside,' she said. She peeled one finger off and immediately I flipped it back on to the gate. It must have been like wrestling an octopus. Finally the head and my mother managed to prise me away from the gate and the head carried me, under her arm, kicking into the school.

After this altercation I was fine, but I like to think that this was a precursor to my future political life – the first of many protests!

I remember very clearly being in the nursery class aged four; it was an old Victorian schoolroom, and it had a big open fire with a guard to protect us infants from falling in. If we were naughty Miss Cross would make us stand facing the fire so that our faces burned. I think about this now and wonder how that would go down with parents if primary schools were to introduce a policy of Stand by the Fire!

I was, I am informed, very bright at infant school. We had little cards that we would write our class exercises on and I'd always be the first up with my card, arm outstretched, 'Finished, Miss!'

One day as I was standing impatiently waiting to be seen by the teacher, I slid my exercise card down the back of a poster on the wall. I'm not sure why I did it: boredom, curiosity, whatever was the reason, it resulted in me receiving a good hiding. I was given the ruler – for that! Mind you, at that time if you had the audacity to go home and say that you'd been smacked you would get smacked again, so I never told my parents that I had had the ruler. They wouldn't go down to the school and defend your corner to the teachers as parents do now. Years later I bravely told my mother I had had the ruler at school and she just said, without looking up from the magazine she was reading, 'Well, you must have deserved it.'

I may have been a bright girl at infant school, but one thing I couldn't do, which Miss Cross seemed to think was essential to the holistic education of her charges, was knit. For Miss Cross, humiliation was the art of education. I remember trying to concoct something with my knitting needles that was probably meant to be a scarf, but that just looked like a tangled mess – quite arty though, I thought. She held it up to the class with a look of disdain – all of my classmates looked on, marvelling at how bad my creation was – and then I got the ruler again! I was only five at the time. Five years old and being burned by the fire and beaten by a ruler for bad knitting was an everyday occurrence at Whiston Infants.

I had my first acting experience at that school. I'd like to say there was the early evidence that it would eventually become my career. That wasn't the case. I remember seeing my parents come into the room and look around, maybe they were looking for me playing Mary, or even a shepherd or king. But no, there I was, standing on a stool pointing at the words with a stick, under strict instruction that I wasn't allowed to sing. At least I'd been given a job, I suppose! I'm still no use at singing. I might on occasion fancy that I can sing but I'm reminded that I can't as soon as the notes leave my mouth. So, Miss Cross, you may have burned me and beaten me but you got one thing right – recognising I was tone deaf from an early age!

We moved from infants to junior school when we were seven. My junior school, Eccleston Park Church of England school, was a mile and a half away and I would walk there and back twice a day, coming home for my dinner. Six miles a day, no wonder we were all beanpoles! One of the tricks of our teachers at junior school was to throw our work out of the window if we were misbehaving. Mr Dean was the worst for it. So we would be standing there, agog as our work frittered through the air. While we were unawares we'd get a great thwack on the back of the legs but not from a ruler this time but a cane; we were seven now, we'd moved on! Then we'd have to hobble into the garden to pick up our ruined work. Thinking back, school really was like running the gauntlet, it's a wonder we learned anything.

When I was in juniors I had terrible bladder problems, something that affected my entire family. Weak bladders were known to run on my mother's side and my poor aunties and mother were martyrs to it. If they laughed they wet their knickers. My dad always said it was a sign of a good holiday if there was a line of knickers pegged out. One time, someone in the family was getting married and my mother and aunties took my grandma to get her outfit from Lewis's, a grand old department store in the middle of Liverpool. Grandma was trying on a particularly smart outfit when she had a fit of laughing at something someone said and laughed so much she wet herself and had to buy the dress.

I was to be cursed with this affliction as a child. In junior school I sat next to a boy called Roger Kelly. He would go on to be an actor himself and changed his name to Sam Kelly. He was in *Porridge* and *'Allo, 'Allo*, among other things. I remember sitting on his desk in a fit of laughter and then the floodgates opening. I would only have been seven or eight at the time. I ran back to my seat; I didn't want to sit down, I just wanted to die. It was awful as a little girl to have that dread of the inevitable humiliation. A hand went up, 'Miss, someone's weed on the desk,' they said with disgust. The teacher made everyone stand up and turn around and then, with all the eyes of my classmates burning into me, I heard, 'Susan Wright, go and get the mop and bucket.' I didn't. I ran the mile and a half to our house and into my mother's arms, crying my eyes out. It was the only time I'd felt able to come home from school and say what had happened to me, I somehow knew that on this occasion my parents would fight my corner. I felt so wronged. I was right – my mother went mad. She understood a weak bladder could be the most embarrassing thing in the world. She went to see the headmistress and defended me to the hilt. And then she went and gave the teacher what for too. It was the one and only time she defended me in school, but it was the right time. I don't think I could have gone back to school after that if my mother had taken the usual parental approach of the day and sided with the teacher. My mother then took me to the doctor's and I seem to remember being given some tablets that sorted it out. But the fact is at that age mud sticks, and whenever a puddle was found in class, from then on the finger was always pointed at me.

Growing up I may not have had any brothers or sisters but I was extremely lucky as there were three other girls in the three houses next door to us who were only children too. That there were four of us in a row, the same age with no brothers and sisters, was a rare occurrence, especially back then. We all knocked about together playing on the street and in our garden – my dad had strung up some old netting he'd acquired for us to play badminton, or 'shuttlecock', as we called it. Dad could always be relied upon to make something out of nothing. A skipping rope, a rounder bat, a tennis racket: Dad was the man to go to.

We were such a tight-knit little bunch of girls. There was Leslie Kruse, who was very clever and went on to Cambridge. My mum always held Leslie up as the person

I could have been if I had applied myself. 'If you'd worked hard like Leslie Kruse,' she would say, 'you could have gone to Cambridge.' This is something I don't believe to be true for a second. Leslie was exceptionally clever and also extremely hardworking and very much deserved her place at the top university. The fact that she was from a working-class background and one of the first women to be admitted to St Catharine's College to study English made her achievement even more admirable. Then there was Valerie Thompson, whose parents I called Aunty Betty and Uncle Joe. Valerie lives in New Zealand now. And there was Frances Rimmer who moved in later than the rest of us. We were a real gang of mates. Valerie's dad Joe who had one leg, and who had so kindly gone to the phone box for me when I scalded my foot, was a whiz on his crutches and would trim the hedges in between the gardens balancing on them. It was a wonder to behold! He never wore a wooden leg although it was rumoured he had one. One day Valerie decided she was going to show it to us and we all crept upstairs. We walked into her parents' bedroom and huddled in tight.

'Sssh!' Valerie demanded. We knew we'd be in big trouble if her mum or dad found us snooping around in their bedroom. We all fell silent as, with all the ceremony that the occasion was due, Valerie reached under the bed and pulled out a long, narrow box. She flipped the locks on the side and we all took a small step back. Then she opened the lid and in unison we let out a piercing scream as we clapped eyes on the wooden leg.

'Be quiet!' Valerie hissed, sure we were going to give ourselves away. 'What do you think it's going to do? Jump out of the box and run round the room?'

We all piped down, Valerie put back the leg, and we crept downstairs undetected.

The four of us would play outside together every day after school and we'd often be joined by a lad called Nigel who lived in one of the police houses on the estate. As a child I don't really remember spending much time inside. Unless it was teeming down with rain we were all ushered out into the street to play and told not to come back in until it was time for tea, and then after tea we were pushed out the door again until it was time for bed.

I stayed in touch with my friends from the street until we left Whiston and went our separate ways, but over the years we got back in contact again and Leslie came to my mother's ninetieth birthday party, which thrilled Mum to bits. It also gave her another opportunity to bring up the fact that if I'd only knuckled down I might have gone to Cambridge and made something of myself.

*

Some of the happiest times in my childhood were during our family holidays. We would rent a seaside chalet in a place called Gronant just outside of Rhyl. North Wales was and still is a big draw for people from the North-West. It's not too far and has some lovely seaside towns. There would usually be a gang of us: Clive, Ena, Charlie and Barbara, Millie, Dave and my cousins, my parents and me. Then others from the family might come along if they could get the time off work that week. There was a bluebell wood near the campsite and a stream where I played in the water with my cousins, when we weren't on the beach building sandcastles. Of course now as I look back it all seems to have been dappled by sunlight, but I'm pretty sure we also had days, if not weeks, of rain where we sat in the chalet and vowed never to go back to Wales again.

We would sometimes hire a caravan when it was just my parents and me. I loved holidaying in a caravan; there was something very comforting about cosying up on a bed that flipped down from an overhead cupboard, while my mother and father turned the table into a double bed. Cosier still was the feeling that we were all together in the same room, playing cards and board games.

When we were holidaying with my extended family they would get all us kids to bed and then the adults would stay up and play canasta. My mother was a demon canasta player, as were all her family, and would often go to the casinos in Manchester, even late in life, and play canasta into the early hours.

A very early holiday was a trip to Butlin's. I was prob-ably only two but it is memorable for one particular reason. We went to the one in Filey. I was on the train that took you around the park and these older girls took a bit of a shine to me and decided that I could be their friend. Mum and Dad seemed to think this was a fine idea. That was until the girls covered me in transfers and swung me around by the arms and they came out of their sockets! I had to go to hospital and have them clicked back in. My mother was very angry about this, declaring that I'd ruined the holiday.

But usually holidays were good times. Another that sticks in my mind was on a farm in Egremont, Cumbria. There was the usual family group and my aunty Josie also came with us. It was haymaking time and they had a young lad on the farm whom we made friends with and who kindly allowed us to get involved in the bailing. Everyone seemed to really click and it was one of those holidays that stands out as so much more than just a week away. Again, it seemed to be sunny all the time.

They would get the hay on the back of the cart and then my cousins and I would climb up and be pulled along, bobbling about on top of the hay, by two carthorses called Blossom and Biddy. After seeing the fun their children were having my mother and her sisters decided that they wanted to get in on the act. The farm hand decided not to put them on the hay but instead to put them on Biddy, the more truculent of the two carthorses. Blossom placidly looked on as Biddy decided to do her own thing, skedaddling off before the sisters were ready. The family bladder weakness took hold and my mother and her hysterical sisters wet themselves and poor old Biddy into the bargain. Another day on holiday ended with a washing line full of knickers.

My childhood really was lovely and I am pleased that I got to tell my mother that I felt that way. My memories as a youngster are something that I'll always treasure and I am thankful to both my mum and dad for creating the kind of environment that allowed me to have such a happy time.

Chapter Two

MY RELATIONSHIP WITH my mother began to change when I was a teenager. Although on the one hand she had been encouraging of my progress at school, on the other she was wary of the fact that I was bright and of where that might lead. Now that I was growing up, she was beginning to view my enquiring mind with suspicion.

I don't believe my mother's attitude to have been malicious, I just think that she feared losing me, she feared that I was outgrowing our family unit, she feared the inevitable day that I would leave home and make a life for myself. My mother wanted to have her family near. Her ideal situation would have been for me to marry a local lad, settle down nearby and have grandchildren for her. But I had ambitions and a life that I wanted to lead. Even though I didn't know that I wanted to be an actress, I certainly knew that I wanted to see a bit of the world, or at least travel a bit further than the end of our road.

My dad was always very encouraging towards my academic success. I think that this is because, in another life, he would have loved to have been a scholar. He had to leave school aged fourteen because his parents couldn't afford the uniform required should he have continued on. He took an apprenticeship as a plumber and later in life went to night school and worked his way up to become a clerk of works at the Ministry of Defence. My father was a very bright man and in lieu of any formal education he educated himself. He had a great love of literature and would recite chunks from Shakespeare. It never occurred to me that this was quite unusual; I thought everyone's dad knew whole swathes of *King Lear*.

Dad also loved books, or at least loved talking about books. I never saw him read, but he knew an awful lot about many great works and he would talk about Dickens, telling me abridged versions of his favourites. He loved *Kidnapped* by Robert Louis Stevenson and I felt like I knew that book without ever having read it. So where my mother was unimpressed about any of my academic successes, my father was always very interested. He wanted me to go to university, to get a degree and have a vocation, to have the opportunities that he hadn't had, I suppose.

My mother was encouraging in other areas. In my teens I was good at sport and Mum really liked this fact. I showed real promise at the high jump and she thought this might be a good thing to pursue. Mum too had been good at the high jump when she was at school and, although she never said it directly, I knew that she was pleased that we shared being good at the same thing. She and Dad wanted me to go on and not only represent the school but to train and be part of the Liverpool Harriers, and so did I until I realised what a commitment it would be. There were plenty of other things going on.

One thing I was quite good at and pursued for a number of years was playing the piano. This was another thing that pleased my mother as she and her sisters had some grand aspirations for their children. It was a very ladylike thing to do – at one stage we were all sent for elocution lessons! I used to attend piano lessons with a lady called Miss Anderson who lived in Prescot, Merseyside. I used to really enjoy playing the piano and I even got to play at the Philharmonic in Liverpool.

On reflection, I think that she was very proud of me that day. I wore a little pink suit with a pleated skirt that I'd been bought to wear at Easter. I had been put forward by my music teacher to play alongside other young people who in turn had been nominated by their teachers, and I played Mozart's 'Minuet in G'. When I saw my mum after the performance, it was clear she had been crying. And for a time she used to tell her sisters, who weren't particularly interested, 'Her music teacher says she's got a lovely touch.'

Then suddenly Miss Anderson stopped taking piano lessons and my mum and dad found a lady in Thatto

Heath, an area of St Helens about three miles from where we lived. I would sit on the bus dreading going to this woman's house. She wasn't as warm and welcoming as Miss Anderson. One day I walked in and she sat me down at the piano and flicked through the musical score book to indicate what she would like me to play. I immediately set to work on 'Für Elise' when she stopped me.

'I've been having a hard time, Susan,' she said.

I nodded, pretending to understand what she was on about. I had that feeling of foreboding, sure that she was about to tell me something better suited to an adult's ears.

'What with the cancer...' she continued.

Uh oh, I thought and began bashing away at the piano keys again.

'Breast cancer,' she went on, undeterred.

I wished that someone would rescue me from this situation. Then, without further ado, she whipped her top up and showed me her chest and the angry scar where her breast used to be. I was very shocked. She whipped her top back down again, as if knowing she had transgressed a boundary. I felt very sorry for her but I feel that at any age this would be very shocking; at twelve it was positively traumatic.

I went home that evening very upset. 'Mum, I don't want to go to that lady any more.'

Mum started into a speech. 'Well, we pay good money for you to go there...'

'She pulled her top up and showed me where she'd had her bust cut off,' I said, embarrassed.

My mother was speechless. When she finally gathered herself she said, 'Right, you're not going there again. I'm not having anyone showing her chest to my daughter, whether it's there or not!'

So that was the last time I had to venture to Thatto Heath for piano lessons and my mother set about finding me another teacher. They found me someone far closer to our house near the Church Youth Club on Prescot Road and I went there for four years until I was sixteen and my interest in playing the piano was starting to wane and the pull of a social life was proving too great to resist.

I started skipping my piano lessons in favour of spending time in the back room of the nearby pub. Instead of using the half crown that Mum and Dad gave me every week to pay the piano teacher, I started spending it on a round of shandies for me and my friends.

One summer there was the church fete and I was there with my parents but I had wandered off and was standing talking to some friends when I spotted them out of the corner of my eye, talking to the piano teacher. She was shaking her head and all three were looking puzzled. If I'd followed their advice and had trained with the Harriers I might have got across the field quick enough to nip the conversation in the bud, but it wasn't to be. By the time I got there my dad had gone silent, something he only did when he was angry or disappointed. My mother took on the admonishment for the two of them and let fly. 'How could you, Susan?' she said, fixing me with a burning glare.

'I'm so sorry,' I said, wanting the ground to open up and swallow me.

'If you'd done it for a week then sorry might be good enough, but six months?'

'I know, I don't know what I was thinking...' I said weakly.

'Well, you weren't thinking, were you? Otherwise you'd have thought that half a crown is a lot of money for me and your dad.' Then she turned to my father who still was silently looking at me with huge disappointment in his eyes. 'Come on, Fred, we're going.' And they left me standing there, to think about the error of my ways.

I was mortified to think that I'd spent the best part of six months spending my weekly half crown on myself and my friends, rather than my piano lessons. I had to pay back every penny of it, having my pocket money stopped for the forthcoming months and I was informed I couldn't have piano lessons again.

I was always on the lookout for a creative outlet and my cousin Lavinia recognised this. Lavinia was a total inspiration to me as a teenager. I was fourteen years her junior, a huge gap at that age, and it was through her that I developed a love of the theatre. Each year on my birthday she would take me into Liverpool to see a play and then for roast chicken dinner at the cafeteria in

Lewis's, the famous old department store. Spending time with an older cousin that I looked up to was something quite special. As a family we did manage to get to the theatre and the ballet quite regularly. I find this remarkable now, as at the time money was extremely tight. But somehow my mother and aunts would find the money to troop us off to the ballet, dressed up and buzzing with excitement. I suppose what else is amazing is that in the late forties and early fifties these very working-class ladies embraced high culture when it came their way. But then again, it was just what that generation did, I suppose. At this time Variety was still popular and people didn't stay in huddled around the TV, they went out to the cinema and the music halls for their entertainment.

Although I had been quite musical (if you discount singing) and I did like to go to the theatre when given the opportunity, the first time I ever really remember being bitten by the drama bug was around the age of fifteen. Until then, acting hadn't been something that I'd thought of as an option. In the same way that we didn't know anyone who had gone off to university, we didn't know anyone who worked as an actor. It just wasn't the done thing for someone from my background. I had always enjoyed English, and had won the school prize for spoken English reading from *Alice in Wonderland* when I was in the third form, but it wasn't until I met my teacher Miss Potter that I realised that I wanted to act. Miss Potter was one of those inspirational teachers that everyone hopes they'll have. She was only in her mid-twenties when she taught us, so she was young and enthusiastic and full of energy. We all loved her. She decided that we needed to perform a school play. Drama wasn't something that was on the curriculum then so any plays that were put on at school depended on the drive of the teacher. The play she chose was *The Tinderbox* and she cast me as the witch. From the day we started rehearsals I knew that I loved acting. I can remember clearly rolling around on the stage as the witch, and feeling absolutely present in that moment. From then on I knew that this was what I wanted to do.

After the play Miss Potter married and became Mrs Sutton. She continually encouraged me to become an actress. I never forgot about Mrs Sutton and the impact she had on me in my school years.

Years later, I was surprised to find myself on *This is Your Life*. My mother had told the producers about Mrs Sutton but they were unable to track her down. I always wondered where she was and how she was getting on, but there just seemed to be no way of finding her.

About twelve months after *This is Your Life* I was asked to present at the Teaching Awards and when I went onstage the presenter began to ask me about teachers that had inspired me as a child. I of course told them about Mrs Sutton. Then a voice that I recognised came over the speakers and I turned around to see an older lady on the screen behind me, sitting at a desk and reading from her diary. 'Today Susan Wright was remarkable in *The Tinderbox* and I hope she'll continue with her acting endeavours...' It was Mrs Sutton!

The next minute there she was, up on the stage with me. I was absolutely thrilled. Afterwards we spent all evening in a bar catching up. She said that she'd followed my career but had never known that I was the Susan Wright she had taught. She introduced me to her husband and we talked about the time we had seen Albert Finney understudy for Laurence Olivier in Stratford. She said, 'Well, of course we all had the hots for him...' As schoolgirls we never thought that our teacher felt the same way about the young actor as we did!

We ended up the evening with the footballer Sol Campbell sitting between us while Mrs Sutton and I stroked his head telling him how beautiful he was. I don't know how that came about, but we both enjoyed it! After that I stayed in touch with Mrs Sutton until she sadly passed away two years ago.

*

I think it is so important to have figures like Mrs Sutton, outside of your family, who can encourage your passions as a child. Parents aren't always the best people to understand why you want to follow a certain path in life. Although my mum did encourage some things that I was interested in, it was in my teenage years that a definite divide appeared between my mother on one side and me and my dad on the other. My mother had always been disapproving and caught up in what other people might think, as if somehow what mattered most was the opinion of the neighbours five doors down whom she'd never really met. My mother was quick to judge and as a result Dad and I forged an alliance as we strived to avoid her scathing criticism. We shared small things, never huge secrets, but it did lead to this air of division between my mum and me and my dad.

That said, if my dad thought that I was out of line, especially with regard to my mum, he would tell me straight. He loved my mother dearly and was fiercely loyal to her. The only reason he ever kept things from her was to not upset her, or at least to make life easier.

There was a lot that we kept from my mother. My dad would say to me as a teenager 'Don't tell your mother' about the slightest thing. My father liked to smoke, but my mother wouldn't let him so he would go to his shed to do it and only I knew.

We knew that if my mother found out that I was going out into Liverpool or seeing a friend she would have something to say about it, put it down in one way or another, so we didn't tell her. We couldn't face the disapproval.

When I was seventeen years old my dad was in charge of my curfew. There were times when he would willingly cover for me. He'd know that I'd come in late but would say to my mum, 'Oh, Sue was in in good time,' and then give me a wink. I felt that me and my dad were a team, and that he understood me. One evening, though, I pushed him too far.

My dad knew what time the last bus back from Liverpool was and that if I missed it then the only other bus dropped me miles away and meant I had a long walk up a dark country lane. One night I had chanced my arm, stayed out a little later than usual, and missed my last bus home. I got off the other bus and ran, my heart pounding in my chest. What would usually happen was that my dad would go to bed, leave the back door on the latch and then I could let myself in and sneak to bed. However, that evening he'd obviously had enough: I was way too late. I got to the back door and pulled but nothing happened; it was locked. I pulled again, still nothing. I stood back and looked at the door for a moment. Surely he wasn't going to make me knock them up? I took a few steps back and looked up at the drainpipe, wondering if there was a way I could scale it and break into my own bedroom. As I stood there, dithering on the step, I heard the bolt being drawn and the door opened. My dad looked at me, with an expression on his face that I dreaded. He was disappointed. He stood back to let me in the house.

'I'm sorry, Dad, I missed the bus and then I had to get the other one, it won't happen again...' I gabbled. The quieter my dad became the more I filled the air with excuses. 'I didn't realise the time, I looked at my watch

SUE JOHNSTON

and it was nine o'clock then the next thing I know it's eleven...'

My dad fixed me with a look that still makes my heart sink thinking about it now. 'You'd better go to bed. And we won't tell your mother about any of this.'

I slunk off upstairs, my tail firmly between my legs. I don't believe I was the most rebellious of teens but my mother and father had high standards and I often felt that I fell below them.

At that age I thought that the gap that appeared between my mother and I was all down to me. Something I had done, something that had changed in me, my yearning for independence. I picked up tension in other people, and thought that if they were upset it was all my fault. It's something I still tend to do now. But, when I think back, my mother may have had concerns that had nothing to do with me.

I was coming up to the age where I would sit my O levels when my mother took a job in a shoe shop and the owner, a widower, was a firm family friend. My parents would go out dancing with this man, together with his brother and the brother's wife, and I remember photos around the house of them all dressed up in their Saturday-night finery. One Valentine's Day, Mother received her usual card from my dad, and another one, from a mystery admirer.

I walked into my parents' bedroom and my dad was crying. I went to say something but then withdrew, it didn't feel right: whatever had my dad so upset was deeply personal. I came out of the room and crept along the landing so he didn't hear me making my retreat. I went downstairs where my mother was standing at the sink washing up. She looked at me.

'What's the matter with you?' she asked.

'Nothing,' I said, shifting my weight from one foot to the other. Then I decided that I really did need to say something, so I dug down deep for some courage. I was hopeless at confrontation, especially with my mum. 'Dad's upset, Mum. I think he's crying,' I said quietly.

Mum waved her hand over her shoulder dismissively. 'Oh he's being daft,' she said. 'He's bought that car,' she nodded outside to my father's new pride and joy, 'and now he's worried he can't afford it.'

She didn't look at me; she just stayed rattling the pots around the sink. I wanted to say that I couldn't imagine Dad actually crying about a car but of course I didn't, I just stood there dumbly.

'If you're not doing anything you can get a tea towel and dry these pots.'

And that was the end of that discussion. Afterwards I felt odd about the whole situation and was left wondering what on earth had really gone on.

After that Dad stopped going dancing but my mother still went. I clearly remember a photograph taken after that time: my dad isn't in it and my mother is standing close to this man.

But Mum's Saturday night dancing didn't last much longer. The friendship, if that's what it was, broke up and the job in the shoe shop came to an end. I have no proof that anything ever went on, and at the time I would never have seriously considered that my mother could have betrayed my dad in any way. But all the same I did feel very very sad for my dad.

Of course, it wasn't something I could ever ask my mother about outright, even when I was much older. We simply didn't talk about such things. And there is always the chance that this was all in my head; I've had a vivid imagination from an early age!

A couple of years on from this my mother became really ill. She had always been a bit of a drama queen about her asthma, but this was serious. She developed pneumonia and had a huge carbuncle on her back, which the doctor had to dress. Eventually the doctors brought in a respirator and my mother was surrounded by tubes and bottles of oxygen. It was a very scary time. Mum was only forty-seven but I felt that there was a possibility we might lose her. Dad would drive all the way back from Liverpool city centre every lunchtime to tend to her, and her sisters came around to make sure she was okay when Dad and I weren't there.

One day, the doctor came round, took one look at my mum and said, 'She needs to go into hospital.'

'What, now?' I asked. He couldn't mean *now*, could he?

'She's very ill,' he informed me and my dad.

Dad prevaricated. My mother was adamant that she wasn't going anywhere so Dad comforted her and told her that it was fine, she didn't have to go anywhere. I looked at them both and then decided that if they weren't going to do anything about it, I would. I went downstairs and called for an ambulance.

As Mum was strapped up and bundled into the back she turned to me and said, 'I'll never forgive you for this!' The idea that the entire street would have seen her taken to hospital in such a public manner was mortifying to her. Never mind that she was at death's door!

I jumped in my dad's blue Volkswagen Beetle and followed the ambulance, its sirens blaring, to the hospital. I was petrified that something was going to happen to Mum. I parked up at the first place I could find to dump the car and ran inside to A&E. Mum, an oxygen mask covering her nose and mouth, was wheeled past me on a stretcher and taken into a cubicle where the curtains were quickly drawn, leaving Dad and me outside.

Feeling terrible, I looked at my dad.

'Don't worry, love, I think she's forgiven you,' he said.

'No I haven't!' Mum's voice floated out from behind the curtain. Dad and I had to laugh.

After this my mum went to a convalescence home in North Wales where she stayed for three weeks. This was much more acceptable to her, there was something genteel about convalescing.

The other thing that must have been going on for my mother around this time, which I didn't realise of course then, was 'the change', as the menopause was referred to (if it was ever referred to at all!).

I think that these things that were going on in my mother's life, combined with a daughter who was spreading her wings and wanting to take on the world, must have contributed to my mother's malaise. She might have had a burning desire to do something that she was never able to because her life had gone down the family route. Not that she ever said as much, except perhaps by referring to me as a 'Michael the Mistake'. I'm speculating, of course, but I do often wonder if there was something else that my mother may have wanted to do. Sadly, this didn't result in her being pleased for me as I sought to fulfil my own ambitions.

I did well at my O levels, but the leap between O levels and A levels was vast, as was the social life that suddenly became available. I left school at the end of the first year of sixth form. My dad really wanted me to go to university and he was fiercely disappointed when I left, but I just knew that there was life out there that I had to experience.

Chapter Three

I LEFT SIXTH form in 1961 and decided that I would get a job and see where things took me. After my first tentative acting steps under the tutelage of Mrs Sutton, I knew that I really wanted to be an actress, but as I had no idea how to go about becoming one, I thought I should earn some money.

My uncle was an inspector of taxes in Manchester and he suggested I might enjoy working in the tax office. My parents were happy about this as they thought that if I took a job I might relent and think about university in the near future. It was also highly respectable and my mother was thrilled at the thought that I was going to be a civil servant. I went to work in the tax office in St Helens for six months and was then transferred to one on Dale Street in Liverpool.

I loved working in Liverpool. The city has always been full of life and energy. The people there know how to have a laugh and the tax office was no exception. Everyone was very friendly and socialised together. The girls I worked with used to go to a club at lunchtime and very soon I was invited along too. In the words of the Marks & Spencer's advert, this was no ordinary club: this was the Cavern, the place that spawned the Beatles.

Although I enjoyed working with the people there, I hated working in the tax office with every ounce of my being. The monotonous drudgery of the job drove me nuts – I was literally paper shuffling – and I was the worst person to be working somewhere as officious as the tax office. I would do anything to avoid filing and would hide post, only for it to be found again days later. I didn't and still don't have a natural administrative bent. Just the sight of a lever arch file can leave me feeling hopelessly disorganised.

We used to go to the Cavern for our lunch break at twelve and return at one. But soon I wasn't returning at one. It became half one, then two, until I was stretching my lunch well into the afternoon and cheating my time card. I remember seeing one of the tax collectors, Chris Crummy, performing there with his band. I nearly fell off my chair and had to hide in order to watch him but he soon left the tax office, when his band the Searchers became successful, changing his name to Chris Curtis. That was the thing about the Cavern. It seemed that everyone in Liverpool of a certain age was down there, being part of it. Even the tax officers! But it was only going to be so long before someone found out what I was up to when I should have been at work.

Around this time I joined a drama group at the

Liverpool Institute. I thought it might be the way into the career I was sure awaited me. However, we didn't seem to learn much, we were just given different things to perform and instructed to go out and perform them. I seem to remember a lot of time on buses, dragging our props with us. Our bookings were usually in old people's homes and the sight of a bunch of extremely keen teenagers ready to bludgeon their ears with 'Getting to Know You' must have made their hearts sink! I made friends with a few of the people in the group but soon I began to drift away. There was no focus in what we were doing and the pull of the Cavern and everything it had to offer proved too great.

I used to love going to the Cavern on my own, taking in the sights and sounds of everything that was going on there. When I first started going it had just stopped being a jazz club but still had the overhang of that jazz/beatnik fashion, tight black trousers and black polo necks, so my attire had to be black – colour would have been far too gauche! I would wear a big baggy mohair jumper and leggings; I thought I looked the bee's knees. The Cavern was on Matthew Street, directly off the main shopping street in the city centre. You walked downstairs, and it was as its name suggested: an underground cavern. As you neared the entrance you could smell the club: it was damp and stinking but it was such an exciting place to be and the smell was part of it.

Once down there it was very dark. There were brick arches that straddled the two cellars that made up the club. It used to drip moisture from the ceiling, and it was hard not to think that it was other people's sweat plopping on your head as you danced. It wasn't unusual to go to the toilet and find yourself face to face with a rat. I'm not painting the best picture, am I? But there was such a buzz about the place that you just wanted to be there. The stage, if you could call it that, was a slightly raised area at the back of the cellars and there were rows of chairs positioned in front of it. To the side of the stage there was a band room where the bands got changed, but there wasn't much cat-swinging room in there either. Down the side of the cellars there was an area where people would stand and do the Cavern Stomp, the signature dance of the club. It was less a stomp than a slowed-down jive. The best way to describe it is to imagine a child doing an elephant impression as they stomp their feet from side to side. Then slow it right down. It was hardly the tango but we thought we looked great!

At the back of the club they served tea and pop. It sounds very naive that we all gathered and drank cups of tea, but it wasn't about getting drunk, it was about the music and the atmosphere, and the Cavern had both in spades. There was a real sense that you were at the heart of something very new and very special.

There is a Cavern club still there on Matthew Street but it isn't the real one. The original Cavern was filled in by Liverpool council in 1973 when they bulldozed the building above. It is mind-blowing to think that such a

hallowed place of modern popular culture had been flat-
tened. But there you have it. Planning and heritage wasn't
big on the agenda in the early seventies.

I marvel at my confidence back then. I would get on
the bus, go into town on my own, and turn up at the
Cavern to see if there was anyone I recognised. I was by
now hanging out there in the evening as well as at
lunchtime. If there wasn't anyone I knew, I'd just make
friends with whoever was there.

When I came home my mother would say in disgust,
'You've been to that club again!' And she was right, I
had, because it had become part of my life and I was in
there every day that I possibly could be. I don't think my
mother could understand why I wanted to spend all this
time with people that weren't my family, so I tended not
to tell her who I was with or what I was doing, which,
when I think of it now, probably added to her feelings
that I was drifting away from her. Of course, I was just
spreading my teenage wings but my mother would trot
out a seemingly endless number of examples of daughters
who were well behaved, who wanted to be close to their
family and settle down. I always seemed to be too independent to her for my own good.

I remember the first time I ever saw the Beatles
perform. It was 1961. I had gone to see the Swinging Blue
Jeans play and supporting them were a group who would
go on to become the biggest band in the world. I have to
say, I lost it – I was mesmerised. There was something so

edgy and vital about their performance that was airbrushed out when they were given their mop tops and their little suits and told to act clean-cut for the teeny-boppers' worried parents. But back then they were going between Germany and Liverpool – they spent a lot of time gigging in Hamburg, honing their craft before they were famous – and they were unbelievably raw and sexy.

I got to know Paul well, and Ringo who wasn't drumming for them yet; it was still Pete Best. I would see John Lennon there with his first wife Cynthia, who I felt was treated very shoddily by the girls who came to see John and were in love with him from afar. I met Gerry Marsden from Gerry and the Pacemakers and his girlfriend, who he later married, and we all became good mates.

The Beatles first appeared on TV on 17 October 1962 on a regional programme called *Scene at 6.30*. At that point my mother knew that they were the reason her daughter spent so much time in the Cavern but she had yet to clap eyes on them. They were dressed in leather biker jackets and looked very sexy. My mum was appalled. After that, when Paul came to our place to drop me off, she'd asked in disgust, 'Has that dirty Beatle been in my house?' She gave me the silent treatment for a while after that.

Paul wrote to me from the Star Club in Hamburg once, a great letter, it even had doodles on the front of it – which was stolen from me when I was working on

Brookside. I took it in one time as no one believed that I had this treasured possession, but then it was whizzed from my locker and I was devastated; no one ever owned up to the theft. My cousin remembers me reading her the letter and what an eye-opener Hamburg evidently was. Little Richard was performing there at the time. There was a dizzying array of people who would come through the doors of the Star Club, Paul said, the likes of which we didn't get much of in Liverpool. He said that in one of the clubs one night John Lennon ended up with a stunning, exotic-looking woman, only to discover on closer inspection that she was a he, which the other Beatles found hilarious.

Another piece of Beatles history I had, which I have to hold my hands up to losing, was an old reel-to-reel of the Beatles singing 'Love Me Do' in someone's garage when they were first putting it together. I am shame-faced to say that I taped over it with the Max Miller show. Whenever I admit this to anyone there is always a sharp intake of breath – I've yet to meet someone who's said, 'Still you're the proud owner of a classic Max Miller show.'

While the Beatles were in Hamburg I began seeing the drummer from the Swinging Blue Jeans, who was still a car mechanic at the time. His name was Norman Kuhlke and he was my first really serious boyfriend. Strangely enough, my mother really took to him. She would make him apple pies to take on tour. She seemed genuinely pleased for me to have a nice boyfriend. Even though he was in a band he was friendly and my mum must have felt I had some stability in this mad Liverpool life she imagined I was leading.

Towards the end of my numbered days at the tax office, Paul McCartney told me there was a job going at NEMS, the record and management company run by the Epstein brothers. When I first started there it wasn't quite the empire it would become; they used to sell a few records and had a furniture shop too.

I was offered a job working for Brian Epstein's personal assistant Peter Brown's personal assistant. I would be his personal assistant. So I was personal assistant to the personal assistant to the personal assistant of Brian Epstein – try putting that on your business card! Epstein would go on to manage the Beatles and give them their signature look. It was a great job, being at the centre of all of the new music that was coming into the country.

One day I had a record land on my desk from America. It was called 'The Hippy Hippy Shake' by Chan Romero. I listened to it and it blew me away. I grabbed the record and went in search of Norman.

'You have to listen to this song,' I told him. 'It's amazing.'

He put it on and his face lit up. The minute the record was finished he went in search of the other band members and that was how the Swinging Blue Jeans came to record their number one hit 'The Hippy Hippy

Shake'. I also told them about 'You're No Good'. I wish I'd asked for a cut of the royalties!

All the groups would come in to listen to the American stuff we received. It was very exciting to be in the thick of all this. My parents were glad that I hadn't gallivanted off anywhere further than Liverpool city centre, but they were keeping a watchful eye on me, wary that if I was daft enough to pack in a job at the tax office I might be daft enough to do anything. When I think about it I must have been a constant worry to my poor parents.

At the time I'm sure my mother and father envisaged that I was up to all sorts but it was all quite innocent. The worst thing we did, I think, was to take something called Purple Hearts. They were given to us by our bosses at NEMS to get us through the night when we had a big record launch ahead of us. If someone had suggested to us that we were taking 'drugs' I'm sure we would have been horrified, but that's exactly what we were doing. These cutely named pills were actually speed, but we didn't think for a moment that we were doing anything illegal.

By the time I was nineteen I had been seeing Norman for over two years. I was still going to the Cavern as often as possible as well as to another club called the Mardi Gras. One night I was out with my friend Bah when I bumped into the tour manager for the Swinging Blue Jeans. This was odd, as I thought that they were all away on tour together – or at least that was what Norman had told me.

'Hi,' I said, trying to be as casual as possible but sensing that something was wrong. 'I thought you lot were on tour.' My mouth had gone dry.

'Nah,' he said. 'Norman's just gone off on holiday to the Canaries with a friend.'

I knew exactly what 'friend' meant. I was devastated. I looked at Bah dumbly, wanting the ground to open up and swallow me. I turned away and ran from the club; I needed to get out of there. I went home and sobbed uncontrollably all night.

The next morning I woke up and just thought, 'Sod it!' I was still devastated by this betrayal but it had galvanised me somehow. I knew that I had to stop living vicariously through other people and get on with my life and what I wanted to do. Norman came back from his week with his groupie, full of remorse. But I was gone; not interested. There were lots of people trying to persuade me to give Norman a second chance, his mother and sister rang me too, but I explained that I wasn't going to get back with him. I needed to look at what I wanted to do, stop literally following the band.

I have to say, even though I was so strong-willed at the time, Norman's betrayal did affect me deeply. Until this point I think I had been entirely trusting and confident, but this experience really knocked my sense of self.

Almost overnight I turned my back on the Liverpool scene. I didn't have any regrets about doing this. The Beatles had moved to London and most of the other bands who had played at the Cavern had also made it big and left. I felt that I had been there for the best part of it. It had been two years of madness, the Beatles had come along and created this phenomenon that was the Mersey sound, and we all genuinely felt like we were part of something special, something that everyone in the country wanted to be a part of. But for me it now seemed the right time to move on.

The last time I saw Paul was when the Beatles came back from London to appear at the Cavern. 'She Loves You' had just hit number one. I was with Paul, then George met us and Ringo came later. We were all going to a party but first we met for a drink. They were all nervous. Since they had left for London they had begun to worry that Liverpool would turn its back on them. That the city would see them as deserters.

'Sod it,' Paul said eventually. 'Shall we go for a drive past the Cavern and see if there's anyone there?'

The gig was the next day but before the Beatles had left for London, people would queue the day before they played to ensure they had seats.

We all piled into Paul's bottle green Ford Classic and headed for Matthew Street. We turned the corner and there was a queue snaking along the street.

'Is this for us?' Ringo asked, craning his neck to look at the crowd.

Matthew Street was so narrow that we couldn't turn round, we had to keeping going. We drove on towards the crowd and as people began to realise that the car slowing down had the Beatles in it, I experienced Beatlemania first-hand. Paul wound the window down; girls were screaming, men were shaking his hand. The crowd surged around the car and it began to rock. I hid under the lads' coats in the back and waited for the fuss to die down. Eventually Paul was allowed to wind his window up and we drove on. I came out from under my pile of coats.

'Well, I think they still remember us,' Ringo said drolly.

We went to the party and that night Paul offered to drop me home. His pride-and-joy Ford began spluttering. Eventually it came to a shuddering halt just outside the abattoir. We both got out and stood for a moment, wondering what to do, until a taxi came our way and we flagged it down. The taxi driver couldn't believe his eyes when he realised he had a real-life Beatle in his cab. Paul accompanied me back home, and we sat up chatting until the early hours – my mum and dad were away and there was no risk of the 'dirty Beatle' being escorted off the premises – and then he went on his way.

That was the last time I saw Paul for many years. He went off to become part of the biggest band of all time and it was time for me to plough my own furrow.

Chapter Four

SINCE SCHOOL MY only real contact with the world of acting had been with the group from the Liverpool Institute. Now that I was determined to become an actress, I set about looking for somewhere that might give me some direction.

I heard that a new theatre was being built by Pilkington's, or 'Pilks' as it is locally known, a large glass manufacturers in St Helens. St Helens was only a bus ride away from Whiston, so heading there for work was only the same as working in Liverpool. Sir Harry Pilkington, the owner of the factory, was married to an actress and their daughter, April Wilding, was an actress too. They were very keen on the arts. The theatre had visiting companies bringing in different shows and I knew that if I could get involved it would be great experience for me. I was also aware that if I got a job at Pilks it would make my parents happy, as the glass factory was seen as a good place to work. So I took myself off to St Helens to secure a job.

I began work in the Pensions Department and immediately joined the amateur group. Of course, I didn't like my new office job that much, but as with the tax office in Liverpool the people I worked with were great. I decided that I needed to tackle this job differently. I was going to come back from lunch for a start! I also decided that even if I didn't like it, no one need know as I was going to approach it as if it were an acting role. Rather than slouch around the place making my discontent felt to all and sundry, I took on my new role of clerk with great gusto, became a whiz at filing and made sure that every single piece of documentation I had to deal with was in order. One of my responsibilities was paying out weekly pensions to past employees. This was the nicest part of the job, meeting the people that you were dealing with. After a few weeks I went along to the first casting for a play that was to be performed at the new theatre and was delighted to be given the role of a cockney maid. All the old people recognised me from pension day and cheered when I came on and there would be shouts of 'Here she is!' I still have the programme from that show, a treasured possession. My parents came to see me perform and they seemed to really enjoy it. There was an article in the *Liverpool Echo* about the show and when my mum died I found it among her possessions. I was really touched that she had cut it out and kept it.

This was a peaceful time for me and for my parents. I had an office job, which pleased them, and I'm sure they thought that once I'd got this acting fad out of my system this job would offer security and a future. For me, I was heavily involved in the theatre and learning all the time so I was very happy. I had such a thirst to learn, to get to grips with everything that the theatre had to offer. I began working part-time at the theatre itself as well as in the office. It became like the Cavern, in as much as I was there as often as possible – it was my new haunt. I would operate the lights and do the amateur shows and work there at weekends, it was a big part of my life.

Around that time I met a very lovely Swiss boy who came to the theatre as part of a touring group. He was the stage manager. In the two weeks that he was there we fell in love in that totally committed, nothing else to worry about way that only young people can. We'd spend the entire time together gazing into one another's eyes. When he returned to Zurich I thought my heart would break. However, he then wrote a very proper letter to my mother and father, care of the theatre, asking if I might be permitted to visit him in Switzerland. We corresponded for some time, but I never did visit him. My mother must have been very impressed by this young man's manners because his letter was another thing I found that she had kept.

Duncan Weldon, the now hugely successful West End producer, was running the Salford Players and he decided to come to Pilkington's theatre for a season away from Salford. He'd previously seen me perform, and it was during his time here that he offered me a job. I would be working in weekly rep as an ASM – acting stage manager.

This would mean working full-time at the theatre. ASM would have been better titled ADB, acting dogsbody! There was a lot of running around involved, but I loved it because, just like when I was working in the NEMS office, I was in the thick of it all. I saw this as a great opportunity so again I gave up a secure job and off I went. I got six pounds a week and paid ten bob on my national insurance stamp. My other job was eleven pounds a week so it was a big cut in wages, something that greatly worried my parents. Also, it was only for three months so there was no future in it – a thing that would make anyone's blood run cold in the early sixties, especially my poor despairing mum and dad. Somehow they managed to grin and bear it. The job was hard work; we were performing one show while simultaneously rehearsing another. From the moment I opened my eyes till I fell back in bed at the end of the day I was working, and it felt great.

At this time, people in the theatre company began to push me to look into going to drama school. A lady called Nelly said to me, 'Now, love, you're a big fish in a small pond here. It's time to go and be a little fish in a big pond.' She knew that if I was going to pursue acting seriously I needed to learn more about how to act, rather than getting up onstage and hoping my personality would see me through. At the time, the only drama school I had heard of was RADA, and that seemed so posh and unattainable for someone from my background that I didn't think I could apply there. However, I recalled that one of the girls from the course at the Liverpool Institute had applied to a place called Webber Douglas in London and had got in, so I decided to apply there.

My dad didn't want to know and refused to even speak about it but my mother, surprisingly, was very supportive and she took me to a women's wear shop where we got things on tick and bought me two outfits for my auditions. This really stands out in my mind, as it was so rarely the case that my mother would be the one on my side while my father was the one who voiced his disapproval. He was very upset by my decision.

I recall being on the train to London in the pink outfit that Mum had purchased for me and feeling like the bee's knees. I had two speeches that I had learned by heart, a modern piece and a Shakespearian passage. For some unknown reason I decided on the way there that I was going to scrap the modern piece and learn something else. I arrived at Webber Douglas a bag of nerves, shaking like a leaf in front of a stony-faced panel, but I gave the audition my best shot.

'Was the hope drunk Wherein you dressed yourself?' I began.

I could hear my accent reverberating around the room. I sounded like Cilla Black! Lord only knows what they made of me. I was terribly nervous waiting for their verdict but I got in! Probably by the skin of my teeth but I was in all the same.

When I returned home really excited by my news I

thought that Dad would come round quickly and be pleased for me too, but he didn't. In fact, my dad was so angry that he refused to sign the forms for my grant, which was necessary for me to attend the school. I think my dad was fearful of the unknown, and for the three of us London was most definitely the unknown. My mother signed the papers, even though she also wasn't too happy about me moving all the way to London. From then on, my dad's anger was directed at my poor mother and she was given the silent treatment.

Years later my dad admitted that he was angry because I just seemed to flit from one thing to another. 'You just get so fixated on things,' he said, 'and then you go cold on the idea and move on to the next. I thought you were going to go the same way with acting.'

This was true of me when I was at school, I did throw myself totally into something new, only to get bored of it quickly and try something else, but I think it's fair to say that acting is something I've stuck with.

After much digging in of heels it became clear that I was definitely going to London. My dad finally relented but he still wasn't happy and insisted that I stay in an all girls' lodging house, which of course was also what my mother wanted.

*

When we first arrived at the hostel in Earl's Court that would be my home for six long weeks, the woman who ran it looked us over and was friendly enough to me and my mother. But she eyed my father and said, 'Men are not allowed over the threshold.' Poor Dad had to wait in the car. My mother on the other hand was much comforted by this woman's draconian approach.

I always find it strange how people can change mood or allegiance at the flick of a switch and usually with my mother you knew exactly where you were, as disapproval was her default position. However, since she had been so good in buying clothes for me and signing my papers, I thought that maybe we had reached a turning point. She would be happy for me to be in London pursuing acting as a career.

I was wrong. My mother looked around the room, her eyes brimming with tears, before saying, 'My life has ended now.'

I couldn't believe she'd said this. That she didn't want me to be in London; she wanted me at home with her. It is sad to think that she found it so difficult to let go of me, and for a long time I was very upset with her for saying this.

My parents said their goodbyes and went on the five-hour journey back to the North-West. I was left in a shared room with a glamorous art student and a young Australian girl who was working in the City. The room was the size of an average double room but in it were squashed three single beds, three bedside lockers, three wardrobes and a sink. The art student kept herself to herself but the Australian would bound across my bed every night like a mountain goat when she returned from her evening follies, crushing my legs. I would politely lie there, wide awake, pretending to be asleep.

Outside our room was a Baby Belling – a hotplate contraption that was a mainstay of cheap bedsit living at the time. There was a meter at the side of the oven and I duly put my sixpence in on that first evening there. I was having a boiled egg, such was the glamour of my first night in London. I wandered off for a few minutes and returned only to find a plethora of pans placed strategically on the hotplate to get the most of this free opportunity. Where was my pan? Pushed to the back, nowhere near the heat. Raw egg for tea. From then on, when I put money in the meter I would watch that Baby Belling like a hawk. Depressingly, it was the same story for the bathroom. Sixpence in the meter and you were given a few inches of hot water, hardly enough to wet your feet. The taps were held together with tights, and then if you left the bathroom for any reason someone would run in and steal your water. If it's a pretty depressing picture I'm painting then that's because it was. It was miserable and I vowed to get out of there as quickly as I could.

After six weeks at college I had begun to make some good friends and two guys on my course told me of a room in their shared house in Notting Hill. I was delighted to be seeing the back of my nocturnal Aussie roommate and the Baby Belling, not to mention the tap tights. When they offered to help me move out I readily accepted. I let the lads in and I bounded up the stairs to get my stuff for them to carry. As they were making their way up behind me I heard an almighty scream – it was the landlady. Some men had crossed the threshold! She pounced on the boys and hurled them out into the street, leaving me to lug my own belongings down the stairs.

From then on things definitely got a lot better for me. My grant arrived, my living situation had improved and my homesickness had subsided. Notting Hill was in the heart of trendy London and I loved every minute of it.

*

The college itself, Webber Douglas, was in South Kensington, a very well-heeled part of London, in a beautiful old building. It was much smaller than I'd imagined it would be, more intimate, and I suppose that was a good thing – I may have been daunted by a huge acting establishment. It was full of extremely beautiful people. There were lots of blond girls with flowing hair who were like stick insects with impeccable diction. I have to be honest and admit that it was such an alien environment to me that it silenced me for the first week. A week may not seem like a long time but that first week away from home, feeling so cowed by my peers that I couldn't even open my mouth, I felt every minute. I felt my accent was so northern that I didn't dare speak. I went to classes and was asked to dance – something I dread to this day – and felt clumsy alongside those gazelle-like creatures. I would be asked to read and I would burn with embarrassment at anyone hearing my accent. I really did suffer from an inferiority complex about my background, but in those days I think most people from working-class stock thrust into a middle-class environment felt similarly to me.

Once I began to settle in and became familiar with my surrounds I realised there was a slight malaise about the place. A lot of the students weren't taking the course seriously – for them, it was just a stopgap between school and the real world or finding a husband and settling down. Back then drama school was often treated by the middle and upper classes as a bit of a finishing school. The principal of the college had been there for years and I felt that his methods were stuck somewhere back when time forgot. But he was about to retire and everything was about to change.

A new principal came in, a man called Ralph Jago. At the same time I was beginning to make friends: there was Mike, a Brummie, and Val who was from Birkenhead, the other side of the Mersey from me, and we clung to each other, northerners in a sea of posh southerners. Val had a boyfriend, Matt, also from Birkenhead, who was in the year above us, and he had a friend called Neil who would eventually become my first husband.

Our class only consisted of twelve people, which was a good number because it was enough to have an audience for any performance you gave, without being too big that you felt you were in danger of being lost in the group. One day we were talking to the new principal. He was really inspirational and when he spoke, we all listened. He asked, 'Can anyone who's working class put their hands up?'

The three of us sheepishly put up our hands, thinking that maybe this was it, we'd been found out finally and be out on the street with our bags following swiftly behind. Ralph Jago pointed to myself, Val and Mike.

'These are the ones to watch, because they are the next generation of young actors with angry, working-class voices.'

It was the time of John Osborne and Harold Pinter, and kitchen-sink dramas like *A Taste of Honey*. *Coronation Street* was already on and suddenly this part of society, my part of society, was being seen and heard in the theatre and on-screen. We were all thrilled with this recognition, and from then on we were all as northern as the Mersey tunnel, laying on our accents thick and thoroughly enjoying the thought of being at the centre of this new wave of modern theatre.

At the end of first year we were all assessed in order to be allowed through on to the second and final year. I wasn't presumptive enough to think that I would breeze through, but I didn't expect Ralph Jago's criticism. He said that he thought he might have to let me go. As far as he could see I was just 'a personality'.

Looking me straight in the eye, he said, 'You can leave here and be a poor man's Pat Phoenix. You'll work, don't get me wrong, but I think you could be a good actress if you worked hard.'

I could feel my face burning with embarrassment. I stuttered something about really wanting to carry on. And it was true. It was all I ever wanted to do.

He allowed me through on to the second year, but I felt that I had to really come back and show him that I deserved my place at Webber Douglas.

That summer I went to work as a ward orderly in a psychiatric unit, or lunatic asylum, as they were still called in those days. I was staying in Lincoln where I had gone for the summer with Neil, who by then was my boyfriend. It was an unusual choice of job but as always I was just trying to make ends meet and any job was better than none. And at the back of my mind I knew that whatever the job was like it wouldn't be dull and it would be grist to the acting mill.

I was charged with varied tasks. I would make up beds, clean, empty bedpans and look after the patients and talk to them. I found it quite upsetting taking these seemingly eloquent people to have their ECT – electro-convulsive therapy to give it its more accurate, brutal name – only for them to return shaken and subdued. There was one lady who was convinced that she was the housekeeper. She dominated the ward and even had keys to the cupboards that she kept hidden under her apron.

The staff had learned to let her get on with her 'job' and she seemed happy with life and her lot. There were also three ladies who were in their seventies but had the mental age of toddlers and I loved spending time with them. They viewed the world with such childlike wonder. We would pack them off to 'nursery' every day and they would all hold hands and walk together. They would then amuse themselves with books and toys. When I think about how frightened my own mother could be in her final years, when she was having one of her delusional episodes, it is nice to look back and think how happy these ladies were. They may have been institutionalised but they were happy and content in their own little worlds. Most of the women in there had had nervous breakdowns of some sort but a few had been there for many years, put into a psychiatric ward simply for having a child out of wedlock. It is so shocking that this sort of thing went on.

I was very interested in everything happening on the ward but soon found myself getting a little too embroiled in the lives of some of the patients. I felt sorry for them – they were locked away, tormented by their own minds – the least I could do was hear what they had to say. I became close to one woman. She helped me change the beds and we would chat. She asked me if I would teach her the twist, which I duly did. A few days later something triggered an episode of psychosis in her and she began screaming and grabbed one of the staff, threatening them. The next time I saw her she was heavily sedated and the whole incident really upset me.

The matron called me to her office and gave me a dressing down for getting too close to the patients. 'It's a fine line working somewhere like this, Sue, don't step over it.'

She advised that I take a step back and do the job without taking it home with me. She was right, of course, she had been there too many years not to know how orderlies should or shouldn't conduct themselves.

By an extraordinary coincidence, once back at drama school after the summer break the new play that we were to perform was announced. It was *Marat/Sade* by Peter Weiss, or to give it its full, not very succinct title: *The Persecution and Assassination of Jean-Paul Marat as Performed by the Inmates of the Asylum of Charenton Under the Direction of the Marquis de Sade.* It is a play within a play and I was cast as Charlotte Corday, a woman institutionalised for suffering from narcolepsy. It was the perfect role for me to show that I could embody a part – I'd just had a full summer of research to draw from.

The role of Charlotte Corday wasn't one I would have been naturally drawn to in my first year as she was very well spoken. It seemed to me that there was always someone else in my year better suited to speaking with received pronunciation, or as we said in those days standard English. But this was what Ralph Jago had meant when he said that I might just become a character actress. I was avoiding taking on the challenge of speaking with a voice that wasn't my own, or inhabiting a character that wasn't close to my own personality, because I was afraid that I might not get it right.

In performing this role I proved to myself that I could rise to the challenge. It was important to keep my own accent and use it when the role deemed it necessary but it was also good to lose myself in this role that was so far removed from myself. We performed the play and it went down very well. I was pleased with my performance and I felt that I had finally got what it meant to be an actress.

I went to Ralph Jago's office the following day filled with trepidation, sure that he would see some cracks in my accent and performance, but he told me that he had been thrilled by it. I was so relieved; I left the room on a high, convinced that I'd finally arrived. I'd like to say that from then on he thought I was the best thing since sliced bread but the very next play we did he shouted at me again for 'just acting', bringing me back down to earth with a bang, and making me realise that I had to tackle every role with the same enthusiasm and understanding of the character as I had with the role of Charlotte.

Ralph Jago was one of the great teachers in my life and there are still things now that he said to me about performing that I try to adhere to whenever I take on a new role.

I thoroughly loved my two years at drama school. To have that opportunity to immerse myself in something I was so interested in was a real privilege. We were taught to sing – as much as anyone could teach me to sing! – to dance and even to fence. It was a real joy to spend all of this time learning the different components of a profession I so desperately wanted to join.

I had mixed emotions when I left college. I was very excited about getting out in the world and trying to make my way as an actress but at college I had been wrapped in the security of the course and my friends and leaving that behind was nerve-racking. There was also the fear that I might never actually get work and I admit that that fear as an actress has never left me. Every time a job comes to an end I feel sick with worry and am quickly convinced I'll never work again.

Now at least everyone is in the same boat, most jobs are precarious and there is no guarantee of a job for life. But in the sixties, most people felt that their job and future was secure and here I was flitting around, ready to embark on a career that by its very nature was short term. My poor parents must have wondered what on earth was going to become of me.

At the end of the final term we performed a 'Press Show' where agents and managers would come to see who they would like to take on to their books. I didn't get an agent immediately but I was offered work in the play *Boeing Boeing*, which was due to tour soon after we graduated. I took this job and I was now ready to go out into the world for the first time as a real actress.

Chapter Five

I WAS TWENTY-THREE years old when I left drama school. I was in one respect extremely independent. I had lived in London for two years and had forged a life for myself that really wasn't expected for a young woman from my background. But when I went back home the fact that I was in London being an actress really didn't matter. The important question was, 'Are you courting?' Getting married and creating a stable family life was still the most valued prize for women, even though some women of my generation were stepping away from this role.

I feel that I was still very much influenced by this way of thinking and instinctively I wanted this for myself. I wanted someone who would love me and validate me. Someone whom I could trust implicitly and who would be my ally in life. When I found out that my first boyfriend had cheated on me it had rocked me very badly. I felt that I had trusted him and that trust had been abused. After that something shifted in me, it was as if I didn't know whom I could trust any more. Even though

I had had a stable upbringing, I think that outside influences such as this were beginning to bruise me. As a result I'm sure I became needy. I wanted to know with absolute certainty that I could trust the person I was with. I now know that trust doesn't work this way, but when I was younger I was insecure and needed reassurance. Neil gave me this reassurance.

I had been going out with Neil throughout drama school and when he moved to Lincoln we still managed to see a lot of one another, even though we were in different cities. I was visiting Neil as often as possible towards the end of my course and it was on one of these trips that Neil bought me a beautiful antique pearl and diamond engagement ring. I was absolutely thrilled.

In those days you were supposed to save up to buy a house before getting married. Neil and I had no money, and acting wasn't a career with steady prospects, but we didn't care. Mum and Dad came to visit and although they smiled and nodded and tried to look pleased, I knew they didn't really approve.

*

When I finished college I was offered the role of understudy in the play *Boeing Boeing*. It was to tour, and this meant a lot of time away from Neil, but we both knew that this was the nature of the job and although I knew I would miss him I had to take this opportunity.

I would be working with the comedian Norman

Vaughan. Norman was a well-known and much-loved TV personality. He had just finished presenting *Sunday Night at the London Palladium* and was hugely popular. I was very honoured to be working with him on my first outing after college. Norman had never acted before but he was a genius at knowing how to get a laugh. He'd say, 'Right, I'm going to stand here and say my first line,' then he'd march over to the other side of the stage. 'Here's where I'll say my second line, then I'll pause,' he would pause for effect, 'and then look back at the audience.' And then he'd say with absolute confidence, 'Then they'll laugh.' And sure enough, he was right. There was a lovely actress called Dory Henderson who played the house-keeper in the play, and Norman would always try to make her laugh but there was no getting Dory out of character, she would just look at him blankly which drew even more laughs from the audience.

We arrived in Torquay for the summer run and Yvette, the other understudy, and I hired a little bungalow together. Neil would come to visit with his brother Geoff and his friends and we had a lovely, fun, sun-drenched summer. I remember sunbathing on the theatre roof on our days off. The stage manager at the theatre was also a fisherman and would take us out on his boat. We would catch our tea and come back and cook it on the beach. Afterwards, we would hotfoot it to the local pub, the Devon Dumpling, where we would spend the evening drinking and chatting. If it was a warm night and we were all suitably equipped with Dutch courage then we would return to the beach to go skinny-dipping!

Max Bygraves was appearing at the theatre next door and I was terribly excited when, through Norman, we were all invited to his and his wife Blossom's silver wedding anniversary. Yvette had a daughter, Deva, who was six at the time and she needed to find a babysitter. 'I've got an idea,' I volunteered. 'I'll call my cousins and see if they fancy coming down.'

So I rang my cousins Bob and David, who were only teenagers at the time, and invited them down to stay. They were both on the train as quick as their legs could carry them: a week in Torquay, away from parental intrusion, in exchange for a night's babysitting? Of course they'd do it.

Bob and David arrived. 'Right lads,' I said as we were leaving for the party, 'help yourselves to whatever, and if there's any problem just come to the party and get us.'

'Everything will be fine,' Bob assured me.

I'm not sure why I took the word of a fourteen-year-old on trust – but I did.

So Yvette and I went off to the party and had a great time. It was such a lovely occasion and great to meet Max who was such a well-known entertainer. The thing that stays in my mind about that party was that they had bread rolls in the shape of the letters 'M' and 'B'. This really was the height of sophistication to me at the time! Afterwards, Yvette and I went for a swim in the sea,

Here I am aged seven

My dad home on leave during
the Second World War

My mum is trying to
cover up my burned
foot, but she's hiding
the wrong one!

My cousins, Pauline and Marjorie, and me in our matching Warrington Walking Day outfits

My mother and her sisters on the poor horse in Egremont

On the sandhills at Prestatyn – my mother is well dressed even here

My first acting role at school, which I loved. The witch in *The Tinderbox*

This was taken in the days when I frequented the Cavern

The drama student

Back home for a visit,
with Whisky the cat

With my first dog,
Woodbine

Following my research at
the National Front
meeting, this was the play
that resulted: *No Pasaran*

My mother on the
day Joel was born

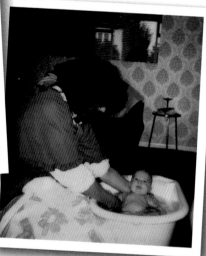

I finally learn to
bath my baby

Joel with his grandad, who he adored

Joel with my dear friend Veron and her daughter Gemma

At Anfield

My *Brookside* family

The remarkable women
holding their families
together during the
miners' strike

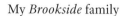

The day we got to play
at Goodison Park, but
were thrashed by the
Grange Hill Girls

thinking that things must be fine back at the bungalow because if the lads had needed anything they would surely have come and told us.

We returned home in the early hours of the morning to a scene of devastation. The first clue was the front door which was wide open but as I strode towards it in panic I nearly tripped over Bob who was lying prostrate on the floor, out for the count. I knelt down next to him then looked at Yvette. 'Bloody hell, Yvette,' I said. 'He's drunk.'

Yvette bolted inside to see if Deva was okay as I dragged my sorry cousin inside. David was in a no better state than Bob, and he was spark out on the couch. I joined Yvette in Deva's bedroom, and found the little girl sitting in bed sipping a light ale! Nowadays social services would have been round in a flash. I packed my cousins off to bed with a flea in their drunken ears and the next day they came down looking very sorry for themselves.

'Sorry, Sue,' they said in unison, their heads hung in shame.

'We drank a load of cider,' Bob added. 'I don't think it agreed with us.'

He could say that again!

Once my cousins were packed back up north, we managed to see out the summer without any more alarming occurrences, but it was soon time to go home.

*

I think if I'm really honest with myself I pushed Neil towards marriage. I wanted him to demonstrate to me how much I meant to him, and I felt that marriage meant a total guarantee of trust. I also wanted to be part of Neil's family. I really loved his mother, Peggy. She was such a carefree woman. I remember we would go back to their house and stay up chatting and drinking and Peggy and her husband would be in bed upstairs. Neil would shout upstairs, 'It's us!'

She'd shout back down, 'Help yourself to whatever!'

She was so laid-back in her attitude. It didn't bother her a bit that we were all there. I loved this as it was so different to being at my mother's, who would have had a fit if I'd turned up late at night with friends. The next morning Neil's mum and dad would sit around chatting to us about what we'd been up to the night before.

I probably inadvertently caused my mother to be jealous of my relationship with my mother-in-law. I think that she felt inched out and also a little insecure around this confident, urbane woman.

Neil and I moved back to London and got a place in Tufnell Park as we planned for the wedding. It was a flat where the landlady lived above us. It wasn't an ideal situation and we didn't have a front door to our flat, just a curtain which she would pull back and march in whenever she felt like it, which was a very claustrophobic way to live.

We were married in January 1967. I had just turned twenty-four. I recently found some footage of my wedding day and have had it transferred to DVD. I don't watch it and wish that things had turned out differently. I just marvel at all the people who are on it who were so important in my life who have since died – to see them brought to life again is amazing. The other thing that strikes me about the video is how happy we all were. It was a wedding day, so I suppose of course we were happy, but to see myself and my family, all looking so young, brought back to life on that day is really very special. I also look at myself and think, 'You're just a girl! What were you doing?'

We didn't have an evening do: we had the wedding and then a spread and a few drinks afterwards and then everyone went home. But I was married and I really don't know what I expected to change for us or what was meant to feel different.

Neil and I returned to London and normal life. I got my second job in the theatre working as deputy stage manager and understudy at the Whitehall Theatre, which is now the Trafalgar.

After a while, the flat in Tufnell Park became very stressful and Neil and I began to argue.

I remember one argument particularly well. I had been working all day and then working at the theatre in the evening and I was really spoiling for a fight. There was no privacy and it was a large open flat. Add an intrusive landlady to the mix, and the fact that we'd had friends staying on the couch for weeks, and it was a recipe for disharmony!

Neil was unwilling to rise to the argument. I had been cooking spaghetti bolognese and eventually I became so enraged that I threw the entire bowl at him. It landed on Neil, and he sat there with bolognese dripping down his front. I stormed out only to return an hour later. Neil was still sitting in the chair with bolognese all over him. We laughed about it afterwards but it was becoming clear that we had big problems in our relationship.

We both agreed that we needed to get out of there for our own sanity. Surely a front door and a bit of privacy wasn't too much to ask? So we handed in our notice and it went down like a cup of cold sick. The landlady was horrible to us. It seemed that she felt deeply betrayed because her tenants were leaving.

We found a place in Wimbledon and moved as quickly as we could. We felt a bit more settled in this new place. By then my contract at the Whitehall Theatre had finished, and I got a job in a toy shop called John Dobbie's in Wimbledon village, a lovely old-fashioned toy store with hand-crafted toys, the kind you dream of as a child but imagine only children in large Georgian houses own. However, as we had started arguing in Tufnell Park, Neil and I found it difficult to stop now we were in Wimbledon. There were still niggles between us and a distance had begun to set in that I wasn't sure we were going to be able to overcome.

Friends began to gently point out that maybe things weren't right between us. I didn't feel the need to confide in Neil about anything any more and I'm sure he felt the same. After months of this we both had to admit that things had come to an end. The marriage just ran its course. It was very sad but, in hindsight, we had married too young.

I remained very close to Neil's family and his mother Peggy took me in when the marriage broke up. His brother Geoff and I were great friends for many years and he was like a brother to me.

I was very nervous about telling my parents that my marriage was over, my mother more so than my dad.

I called home, and spoke to my father; I was very upset.

'Dad, Neil and I have split up,' I explained.

There was a long pause and then he asked, 'Are you all right, love?'

Through my tears, I managed to blurt out, 'What will Mum say?'

'Come home, love. I won't say anything until you get here.'

So I headed home, feeling dreadful but knowing that my dad was on my side. My mother wasn't thrilled by the notion that her young daughter was to be a divorcee. I don't think we even knew anyone else who was divorced at the time. There I was again, breaking new ground! Mum held her counsel for a little while but then couldn't help a round of 'I told you so's. She was very upset for me, and was wondering what would become of me, I suppose her concern was that no one else would want to marry me again, that I'd be left on the shelf. She was also worried about what other people would think.

There was a family party that weekend. 'Don't say anything when we get there,' Mum warned me. So that evening I had to do the rounds and smile while everyone asked me how Neil was and how life in London was treating me, when all I wanted to do was go home and cry. I came away from the party annoyed and embarrassed.

'I'm not coming back again, Mum, until everyone knows. It's not on, ' I informed her.

My poor mother. She really didn't want the job of telling everyone I was getting a divorce but if she wouldn't let *me* tell them the truth, then she would have to.

Not long after the marriage ended, I discovered that I was pregnant. I was very scared and wasn't sure whom to turn to, so I called my dad and told him. I said that I didn't know if I could have it, how would I cope? Dad went very quiet on the other end of the phone. The idea of contemplating an abortion in those days was extremely controversial. It must have been very hard for Dad to hear this from his only daughter, especially when I was so far away and in such a predicament. Dad eventually said, 'Well, you do what you need to do, love.' I knew that I had my dad's support in whatever happened and this meant the world to me, I wasn't on my own. Then he said quietly, 'Let's not tell your mother.'

I agreed that Mum didn't need to know this right now, and I put down the phone. I was still in a total bind and didn't really know what to do, so for a little while I did nothing. A few days later I miscarried. At the time I was relieved. Relieved I'd not had to make a decision, relieved that I didn't have to be a single mother at the age of twenty-five. I felt that I could move on a little now but these things have a way of staying with you.

*

I had moved into Peggy's after the marriage ended. I felt safe there, and still considering myself to be one of the family. I began working at a pub on the Thames in Shepperton called the Red Lion, and the great atmosphere and camaraderie of working there buoyed me up for a time.

I got to know the customers well. One of the regulars was a man in his fifties. He would begin the evening chatting away pleasantly, and seemed to all intents and purposes a lovely man. He would begin with beer then move on to spirits and a mixer, then he would dispense with the mixer and drink more and more until he was completely paralytic. I had never known anyone get quite so drunk.

'You know, Sue,' he said to me one day, leaning in and waving his empty glass towards me, 'you know something?' he repeated again, as if gearing up to impart some immortal words of wisdom.

'What?' I asked, smiling at him as we had been having a great laugh as the night had gone on.

'You've got a lovely face.'

I smiled awkwardly and served the bloke next to him.

'No, really,' he said, as if everyone had disagreed. 'You have! It's such a shame about that nose, though,' he added, waving his finger at his face to indicate where my nose was, should I not have realised. 'Spoils it. You really should get a nose job.'

He plonked himself back on his bar stool and his mind wandered to his next drunken thought.

The man I was serving paid and slunk away, embarrassed. I was devastated. How could he say something so personal? The landlord had been serving someone else nearby and had heard what the drunk had said. He lifted him from the stool and ejected him into the London night. But it was too late; I was in floods of tears. This comment was like a spear to my heart. I was so low at that time, living with my mother-in-law but knowing it couldn't stay that way for ever, still grieving the end of my marriage and dealing with the miscarriage.

This man's cruel jibe stayed with me for years and years. I suppose it still does, if I'm honest. In fact, it came back to haunt me last year when I had something written about me that was so hurtful that I felt the same pain again.

Last year I was on steroids for my back and had put on weight. I had gone up to eleven stone, which is very heavy for me. It was during the time I was filming *A Passionate Woman*. I am immensely proud of that drama but I find it hard to look back at because my face looked so bloated by the steroids.

Then something compounded my self-consciousness to such a point that if I hadn't been working on *Waking the Dead* and had to go into work the next day I might have given up acting altogether.

It was the day of the London Marathon and I had been invited by Ian McKellen to go and watch the marathon from his place in London. I had bought the *Observer* that morning and I was having a quick flick through when I came across a large picture of me and Alun Armstrong – who played my husband in *A Passionate Woman* – and underneath it was the line, 'Sue Johnston looked confused, but wouldn't anyone with a pair of tennis balls lodged in their cheeks?' The writer then went on to mock how I looked, being extremely personal.

I was devastated. I already thought I looked at my worst, but for someone to pick up on it and make such an issue of it was extremely hurtful. I didn't want to leave the house. Frances Barber, who had played my sister in the drama, had read it too and she was extremely supportive.

'Sue, you have to try to ignore it,' she said.

'I can't ignore it. It's so awful,' I replied, feeling that everyone in the country must have read it by now.

'They don't think they're writing about a person when

they write these things,' she said, trying to comfort me. 'They just think that as you're on the telly you're fair game.'

It didn't feel fair. I didn't want to be fair game to some critic.

Without me asking anyone to do it, people emailed the editor of the *Observer*. My friend Susie emailed the critic in question, telling him in no uncertain terms what she thought. He emailed her a rather curt response back. 'Right!' she said angrily. 'He's going to be getting a little present from me!' And she marched off to buy two tennis balls. She parcelled them up and I saw her writing a note.

'What are you doing?' I asked.

She held up the note that she was about to post along with the balls. It read, 'Shove these up your arse!'

I like to think that I'm made of tougher stuff, that I could weather something like this, but it just makes you feel vulnerable. The critic did issue an apology the week after, and I was very grateful to everyone who complained on my behalf but I was still very shaken by it.

Attacks on one's appearance are so personal that I think it is hard to ever shake them off. It certainly is for me. The nose comment from the drunk in the bar came at a time when my self-esteem was on the floor. I really needed some help: I was allowing things like this man to get to me and I felt that the grip I had on myself was getting looser day by day.

One evening, Peggy threw a family party and one of her relations asked rather cuttingly what I was doing there when I was Neil's ex-wife. I felt devastated. I realised it was time I moved out and stood on my own two feet, even though I didn't feel ready for it.

*

I felt like I had failed, that my life was beginning to move off into uncharted territory and I wasn't quite sure how I'd come to this point. I needed some control, and the one thing I knew that I could control was food. I performed in a drama at a summer school around this time and I was talking to the director about a part that I would quite like to play.

'Oh, you could never play that part,' he said flippantly. 'You need to be thin to play that role and you'll never be thin, you're big-boned.'

Again, this comment really affected me. I was upset at the idea that I would never be tiny and left thinking 'Who is he to tell me what size I can be?'

After the summer school, I embarked on another theatre tour and while I was away I stopped eating. When I did eat it was in a very controlled way. I would have a pork pie and a Scotch egg at lunchtime and then nothing until lunch the next day. I don't know why I chose those two things, but I don't think that matters, the fact was I had begun to ritualise my eating habits.

This obsession with food, or control of what went in

and out of my body, wasn't something that I'd had when I lived at home with my parents. It was something that had crept up on me since college.

It is interesting to think about where the seeds of body consciousness are planted. As a teenager, I never thought about my weight or my figure; I'd always been happy with the way I looked. I was an average weight. I never went on a diet. We'd have fry-ups for breakfast, a lunch that consisted of whatever my mother put in front of me, and dinner at night. I was very active, expending energy all the time. At school I walked there and back. I was always out playing in the street as a little girl and then as I got older I would be out dancing till all hours. Food wasn't something I worried about; it was simply fuel for my body.

My mother would occasionally tell me if I put on weight, and if I lost it she'd say, 'Ooh, you look thin.' She wasn't frightened of telling me that my hair looked a mess, I could do with putting on some make-up, or that I should stop dressing like a boy. But my mother never fanned the flames of what would eventually become an eating disorder.

I can remember clearly when food became an issue for me. While at college, Neil and Matt had gone away on tour for a few weeks, and Val came in one day waving a piece of paper with some instructions on it.

'Look at this!' she said excitedly. 'It's the grapefruit diet. We should do it while the lads are away. We'll look great by the time they get back. Surprise them.'

'What's the grapefruit diet?' I asked. I'd never heard of it before.

'Well,' she said, scanning the instructions, 'you have a grapefruit before every meal.'

The look of the moment was led by the likes of Jean Shrimpton and Twiggy, and around the corner from our college Biba had just opened their first shop, which was full of little slip dresses that were to die for. Being skinny seemed like a perfectly normal thing to want to be.

'And that's it? I can eat what I want?' I asked, thinking about having grapefruit then pie and chips, yet still managing to slink down the road a size eight. This diet was some sort of miracle, I thought for those few short moments, why had no one discovered it before!

'No,' Val said, looking slightly downcast as she delivered the disappointing truth. 'You can have an egg for breakfast, some turkey for lunch and a bit of ham for tea. Oh, hang on,' she said, her face brightening. I leant in – what was it? Crisps? I wondered, or maybe a cream cake? 'You can have some veg,' she said flatly. My face fell.

So this was a classic high-protein diet. And having never dieted before in my life, at the age of twenty-two I embarked on the grapefruit diet. Val and I stuck to it religiously and miserably and when the lads came back we had lost over half a stone each.

Of course, after a few weeks of eating normally, I was back to my old size and my Biba dress was confined to the wardrobe. What I hadn't realised was that I had begun the never-ending diet cycle.

*

The tour took us to Gillingham and I had a particularly unhappy time there. We were staying in high-rise blocks near the precinct in the city centre. There was a large municipal swimming pool nearby which would become my haven from the oppressiveness of where we were staying. For some reason we weren't allowed to congregate in each other's flats so the only place we could socialise was at the precinct and the pool.

One day I had taken myself off to the swimming pool and while I was there a child drowned. It was so awful, and although there was nothing that I could have personally done about it, it hit me really hard. I couldn't stop thinking about this poor child and his poor mother. This event compounded my homesickness, how low I felt, and the awful flats that we were staying in added to this further. I stopped eating practically altogether and got thinner and thinner, still feeling that it was something that I was in control of in a world where everything else was out of my hands, where children could die under the same roof as me and I was powerless to stop it.

When I left Gillingham I went back to the theatre where the director worked who had said that I was big-boned. He didn't recognise me, I was so thin.

My skinny frame was shrouded in an oversize jumper. The director looked at me in horror but I felt triumphant. 'See, I told you I could be thin.' Like it was some kind of prize.

I didn't think it at the time, but the break-up of my marriage had hit me hard and I was trying to rein in my life in any way I could. I wasn't sure what to do next or what direction my life should take, and even though I was managing to work as an actress I felt very alone and rudderless. It would be a long time before I felt like I got back to being me again.

Chapter Six

IT WAS THE late sixties and the world of theatre was transforming. Politics was seeping into not only the performances but in the way that theatre companies were being set up. Small co-ops were springing up that would survive hand to mouth until they proved to the Arts Council that they were worthy of a grant. A lot of these companies were doing cutting-edge work and I wanted to be part of this.

The Portable Theatre Company had recently been set up by David Hare and Tony Bicât. David is now one of our most acclaimed playwrights. As time has passed it had become part of modern folklore that David was an 'angry young man', one of the new breed of directors, railing at the establishment, that Ralph Jago had referred to back in college. I can't say that I saw much anger, if I'm honest, he was just a genuinely lovely director and writer to work with. But I suppose at the time we were all angry in a sense, if angry means unwilling to accept the place that our class deemed we should take in life.

That said, we were based at Tony's mother's house off Charlotte Street in Fitzrovia, a well-to-do part of London, and I ended up renting a room there for a time. It was a very grand place to be for an impoverished actor; we were hardly down t'pit!

We managed to get our hands on a clapped-out Volkswagen van to tour in and off we went around the country. My first role was as Madame in Jean Genet's *The Maids* and after that we performed a number of different plays, with David writing some to throw into the mix. We would often find that we struggled to pay ourselves a wage, and the places we played weren't exactly packed to the rafters. On one occasion, in Coventry, we played to an audience of two, which was pretty depressing.

I met up with David some years later when he was very much established as a great playwright. He said that despite the fact that we often found ourselves playing to one man and his dog, there are hundreds of people who claim to have seen those plays. They must have snuck in because we didn't see them. That said, we did have a number of successful shows. We opened David's first play, *Slag*, at the Canterbury Theatre and it was really well received. I felt that I was part of something fresh, that we were doing stimulating work.

Although David wasn't quite the angry young man everyone would have him be, he was extremely well read and was the first person I'd met who brought an intellectualised way of looking at politics, it wasn't just a gut reaction for him. I was very emotionally driven in my politics; any sense of injustice had me up in arms. David had a way of contextualising politics, of showing me that my beliefs actually had merit and basis. I suppose he was the first person who showed me that having a strong political opinion didn't mean that I had to lose my rag. That my political beliefs could be expressed in a methodical and rational way.

At the Portable Theatre Company, I still had one eye on my weight. I was convinced that I was too big and that I needed to do something about it so I went to the doctor's to see if I could procure some slimming tablets. I told myself it was because I was attempting to give up cigarettes and didn't want to put on weight, but as anyone who has had the eating demon in their head will tell you, it wasn't just to manage my weight without cigarettes; I wanted them to make me as thin as possible.

The doctor gave them to me and I went home and popped my pills. I completely lost my appetite, I smoked like a chimney – so much for that – and I cleaned the house from top to bottom. I had been prescribed amphetamines. When my packet of pills ran out I went back to the doctor's like a junky after their next fix.

I walked through the door into the doctor's room and said breezily, 'Hi, Doctor, I've just come to get some more of the pills you prescribed.'

'I'm sorry,' he said, looking at my notes, 'I've been told that I can't prescribe those tablets any more.'

I felt a stab of anxiety but tried not to show it. 'There must be a mistake, Doctor, the pills you gave me were working really well, they were fine. And I just need some more.'

'I'm sorry, Susan, but we can't give them out on prescription,' he said, looking sorry for me.

My bottom lip began to quiver. 'But the thing is, Doctor, I'm an actress and I have to keep an eye on my weight and...' I launched into a pathetic story of why I needed these tablets. As my pleas became increasingly desperate, the doctor put his hands up to appease me.

'Just wait here, Susan,' he said and quickly left the room.

I sat in the chair, wondering where on earth he had gone. Had my histrionics been so bad that he had to leave the room for a break? About what seemed like ten minutes later he came back clutching a paper bag. He handed it to me.

'Here you go,' he said quietly. 'And don't tell anyone you got them from me. You'll have me struck off.'

This is shocking, really, when you think about it, a doctor handing over slimming tablets to a desperate young woman. However, I know there was something very manipulative in my behaviour that day. Something that with hindsight was a warning bell for how gripping my obsession with food would become.

*

After two years with the Portable Theatre Company, I met a director called Malcolm Griffiths, who had just been appointed by Farnham Theatre Company. He asked me if I would consider joining him. The actors and the production team at Farnham were all on equal wages and the idea of a steady fair wage was hard to turn down, so off I went. Malcolm wanted to do great, experimental work and he was a fantastic director. We were performing plays such as *Look Back in Anger*, where Matt from drama school – now my friend Val's husband – played opposite me.

I was living above a pub just around the corner from the theatre and once again I threw myself into theatre life. Malcolm continued to introduce new plays and new ways of directing. When he told us that we were to perform *Much Ado about Nothing* we were all excited to see what his take on Shakespeare would be. Malcolm was very progressive, and the fact that he had set up a cooperative had worried some of the people on the board of the Farnham Theatre Company. When he decided to stage *Much Ado* with an avant-garde twist, it was too much for the traditional theatre board and they told Malcolm that his contract would not be renewed. We were a cooperative and everyone felt very strongly that if Malcolm was going to be made to leave, then we would leave too.

Several of us had made our homes in Farnham and now had nowhere to go. We decided to move back to London and a few of us, including actors Maev Alexander and Denis Lawson, shared a flat in Chiswick. On the surface I was happy to be moving back to London, but I think that the despondency I'd been feeling throughout my twenties was now magnified by the move.

I began to spend more and more time on my own. I would get home, take to my room and get under the bed covers, not coming out for days. I had taken to painting everything black: my bedroom was filled with bottles of flowers and I had painted both the bottles and the flowers black. It seemed like a perfectly normal expression of how I felt at the time. But my friends were beginning to worry about me. I finally took myself to the doctor's.

'Is there a history of depression in your family, Sue?' he asked.

Depression? I was shocked by the word. Surely I wasn't depressed. There must be some more plausible explanation for why I felt so terrible. 'No, of course not…' I began, but as soon as the words came out of my mouth I knew that that wasn't true. Depression – or at least a propensity to be despondent – had been with me for as long as I could remember.

Mum would say, 'What have you got that face on you for? You need to cheer up, everything you've got, you should think yourself lucky.'

My mother very much belonged to the school of thought that says that everything can be solved by pulling your socks up and getting on with life. But even as a teenager I knew that there was more to it than just tugging at the tops of my socks. I used to write in my diaries about the way I was feeling but the fear of my mother reading them was so great that I would write in code. Months later, when the black fog of depression descended again, I would go back to my diaries to see how I had felt last time, only to find I couldn't decipher my own code!

I knew that my dad and other members of his family experienced a similar malaise from time to time. My dad was very sensitive, and when he was upset about something he felt it very deeply. I cannot say for certain that he suffered from depression but I do know that this is how *I* often have reacted to things over the years. We didn't talk about things like that when I was growing up. He would be very quiet during these times and I would know that it was just one of those periods that Dad went through. It was only as I got older that I realised that my feelings of despair were similar to those of my father.

So I told the doctor that yes, I thought that maybe there was depression in my family. He prescribed anti-depressants, and I went home feeling like I'd somehow just let the family cat out of the bag.

I have heard it described as the 'black dog' and over time I came to understand why this is. Depression is a malevolent black presence, always stalking you. Something that you have to be forever on your guard against. It was like something was constantly on my shoulders, weighing me down.

*

The tablets took the edge off my depression. It was still there underneath, but I now felt up to getting a job in a pub called the City Barge, next to Kew Bridge on the Thames. I loved working in a pub again. I got to know the regulars and quickly began to feel at home, but I think my friends still viewed me as something of a lost soul. One of them, Peter, a friend from Farnham, came to me with an offer. I think he wanted to help get me back on track.

There was a new arts centre in Marylebone called the Cockpit and Peter had got the job running it. He asked me if I'd go along too, but to open a coffee bar for them. It would be a stopgap, I decided, and at least I would be working in a theatre environment, so if any opportunities arose I'd be there to take advantage of them. I went about the venture with great gusto: I decided I would make fresh soup and cakes and hot meals, all from locally sourced foods. Of course, at the time we couldn't have advertised it as locally sourced food, people would have thought we were mad. 'What – you bought it from the market? What do you want, a medal?' But I like to think of myself as a pioneer in the whole foods world! In fact, I used to go to the market round the corner from the theatre on Church

Street in Marylebone and became very close to one of the traders there, a lovely man who took me under his wing. One morning he took me to Covent Garden, where all the market stall owners from around London still came for fresh fruit, veg and flowers. You had to be there early to get the best stuff, so I had to set off at 3 a.m. to witness this London institution first-hand.

One of the groups being run at the Cockpit was headed up by Gordon Wiseman. I was very interested in the work he was doing: using theatre to teach children with special needs. He then went on to set up a Theatre in Education team for all schools. I would sit in the gallery watching as he worked and had lengthy discussions with him about his methods. I let slip that I was an actress and soon he was allowing me to join him in the discussions with the young people he was working with. Eventually there was a vacancy for a new member of the team so I auditioned and got the part. I'm sure that I'd gone on at the poor man so much that he felt he had to give it to me! Either way, it was the start of an exciting new chapter in my life.

Part of Gordon's brief was to perform set texts that were on the school curriculum for fifth and sixth formers. The funding for this group came from the Local Education Authority, so he wasn't allowed to develop any extra-curricular work, which was fine for a time, as the way in which he worked with these texts was fresh and innovative. Observing how he took the text apart and presented it to these young people in a way that they could understand it really appealed to me, and it was the beginning of my huge love affair with Theatre in Education, or TIE.

For anyone not familiar with TIE, put simply it is bringing theatre into schools to use as an educational tool. At a basic level, it is just another way of teaching children, but I think that when it is at its best it is capable of transforming lives. The response from students was phenomenal. Many children never go to the theatre as it is often seen as a solely middle-class pursuit, but from my experience I firmly believe that all children of all backgrounds respond positively to theatre when it is performed in an engaging and non-patronising way. And the fact that Theatre in Education groups are mostly peripatetic also helps. Young people always seemed to open up more to us as outsiders than they did with their teachers.

The first play I worked on was *Romeo and Juliet*. We performed it as a play within a play, so that the young people would come into it as the extras and I – I was playing the director – could manoeuvre them easily around the action. They were part of the scene at the ball where Romeo and Juliet meet, and they were all given either a Montague or a Capulet colour when they came in, so they had a ready-made allegiance. I remember that the music by Andrew Dixon was fantastic and there was such an element of fun about the whole performance that they would all be buzzing with excitement when we broke for lunch.

In the afternoon they would come back into the theatre, expecting more of the same upbeat fun, only to be presented with two coffins: Romeo's and Juliet's. They would then have to discuss why they had died and how they thought that it had been allowed to happen, using the text to back up their argument. The young people were always engrossed, because they had invested time in the characters and the play, rather than reading it at their desks. I spent two years at the Cockpit and I learned so much from both the people in the theatre company and the young people we worked with.

This time was a real hiatus. My friends from the Cockpit and I would go to a pub in Marylebone opposite the theatre. The locals were real Londoners and looked on with bemusement at us arty-farty types frequenting their pub. However, one evening this all changed. There was a power cut and huddling round candles brought out the Blitz spirit in all of us and soon we were chatting away like old friends. After that there was no division between the locals and the actors, we were all bar buddies.

Some of the men that we befriended were – to put it mildly – treading on the wrong side of the law. One evening, one of these guys approached me. 'Here, Sue,' he said, checking that no one was overhearing our conversation. 'Fancy earning two hundred quid?'

Of course I did. Two hundred pounds was a lot of money then and I was skint.

'Go on...' I said, intrigued.

'We need a posh bird to go up West.'

'I'm not posh...'

'You can do posh, though. Anyway,' he leaned in, 'alls you have to do is take this credit card, go into Harrods and buy as much gear as you can carry, then bring it back to me.'

He didn't need to explain that the credit card was hooky. That night I couldn't sleep. It was a very tempting offer as I was on baked beans for the fifth time that week but I just couldn't do it. I was nervous going back into the pub the following night.

I approached my prospective partner-in-crime. 'I can't do it. I'm sorry.'

'No problems, love. Don't worry about it,' he said.

I think that is as close to dealings with the underworld as I've ever come!

But then something was to happen that made my newly regained sunny outlook and love of London come tumbling down.

*

One night I was heading home on the tube. It was 7 November 1970. I was twenty-seven. I'll always remember the date. I got off at Gunnersbury Park tube station with the usual crowd but had to stop to pick up a prescription.

When I came out of the chemist's, the place was deserted. I opened the gate to take me along the lane, under the bridge – the path I usually took. I felt vulnerable but I'd committed to taking this way home so I carried on.

I heard a noise behind me that made me turn around. A young man was leaning back against the fence and was doing something I couldn't quite make out at first, then I realised he was masturbating. I stopped momentarily, shocked by what I was witnessing, then I began to run.

I heard him thundering along behind me and I was panic-stricken. I knew he was going to try to attack me. I threw down my bag, thinking that he might just want the contents of my purse and hoping that he'd take it and leave me alone, but he lunged for me, grabbing my throat. He punched me in the side as his fingers squeezed into my neck. Everything went into slow motion.

'I'm going to die now,' I thought.

I heard screaming, it seemed to be coming from far away and then it came nearer until I realised it was me. I was screaming for my life.

I suddenly began to fight back with every bit of strength in me. I was kicking and clawing at him. At that moment the fact that he might be about to rape me hadn't crossed my mind: I was simply fighting for survival. He stopped and hovered over me, staring straight at me, spitting bile – as if sizing me up. I'm not sure if he heard something that disturbed him or was deterred by the fight I'd put up, but he ran off, leaving me scrabbling to pick myself up. It was all over.

I picked my bag up and ran. He had punched me everywhere but at that moment I didn't feel any pain. I was too terrified he might be waiting around the corner. I had a good friend, Kathy, who lived on the estate next to the station so I ran to her house and hammered on the door.

'Oh, Sue…' she said pulling me in, shocked to see the state of me.

'I've been attacked,' I said and then burst into tears.

'Come and sit down,' Kathy said, guiding me gently over to the settee.

Kathy's husband and brother-in-law came into the room. They took one look at me and knew that I'd been attacked. I couldn't look at them.

'What does he look like?' Kathy's husband asked.

I could only describe my attacker's clothes. They shot off in the car to look for him. Kathy went in the kitchen to make me a cup of tea. I was sitting, numb, perched on the edge of the settee. I felt something trickling down the leather material and onto the floor. I looked down and realised I had wet myself.

Kathy came back in, and if she noticed, she didn't say anything.

'Don't worry,' she said kindly and took me upstairs. 'Let's get you cleaned up.'

She put me in the bath and I scrubbed myself clean and changed into some of Kathy's clothes, which of course I shouldn't have done as the police wanted to examine me when they arrived. Kathy's husband had called them. They put me in the back of the panda car and drove me around to see if I could spot the man, but I couldn't see him anywhere. They asked me to describe him, but even though I could see him in my mind I found it impossible to pin down anything about him. I went home that night terrified.

After this I totally lost the plot. I couldn't go into work. I began suffering from severe migraines and was prescribed Valium. I was still fearful of being attacked and had to walk down the middle of the road when I went out, obsessed with being visible to other people should I be attacked again. One day, I was walking through Waterloo Station when someone ran up behind me. They were running for a train but I crouched on the floor and went into hysterics. I was an absolute mess.

My friends tried to get me to talk about what had happened but their kind words had the reverse effect on me and I began to close down entirely. I was in desperate need of some help but didn't know how to ask for it. I didn't tell my parents what had happened as I really didn't want to worry them. I knew that me being attacked in London was the sum of their fears. I wanted them to think that things were going well for me, even when I was at rock bottom.

*

Fortunately, my friend Jude, the secretary at the Cockpit, asked me if I'd like to move into a flat with her and her partner in Maida Vale. Living with Jude, I was able to start putting what had happened behind me, and living with her was one of the happiest and most peaceful times in my life. We lived in an apartment at the top floor of an old Georgian house. It was owned by a designer, so everything about it was well thought out and it was a pleasure to live there. I cycled to work each day and I felt like I was beginning to be able to breathe again, that the attack was behind me and my depression was lifting.

I look back at that period in my life, the attack and the subsequent trauma, and feel that it was one of my darkest times. But I came out of it, and things changed and improved for me when I was able to help myself again. I have learned that whenever things are really bad something good is always around the corner. It just might not be the first corner that you come to.

Chapter Seven

I WAS STILL very much in love with TIE but my love affair with London, for the time being, was over. I felt that I needed to move away from the city, and that the anonymity of the place wasn't helping me. As a Theatre in Education team we would meet up with other TIE companies to find out what people were up to in other parts of the country and to share best practice. At one of these meetings the TIE group Coventry Belgrade put on a demonstration that had me transfixed.

Coventry Belgrade was at the forefront of TIE, performing their own original work and breaking new ground as they did so. They performed one of their programmes for infants called *Pow Wow* for us, and a section of a play about the Protectorate period or, as they termed it, the Civil War. I had never heard it called the Civil War before. Both pieces were thought-provoking, putting the events in a social framework and drawing parallels with the modern world, but allowed the children to reach their own conclusions.

The performance and energy of the company really

inspired me. I left feeling that I would do whatever I needed to move up to Coventry and work with this fantastic theatre group. I wanted to still work with kids but I wanted it to be relevant; to take something historical and give it a new viewpoint was quite revolutionary at the time as history was still being taught in an Imperial context, placing an emphasis on the conqueror's view of history. Also, Coventry Belgrade was aimed at children of all ages, not just secondary school kids, and they weren't married to the curriculum texts as we were at the Cockpit. I was thrilled when I was offered a job there.

Having the opportunity to start again was a relief for me. A new place where I could establish new friendships and a new life. The actress Maggie Steed and I were friends and we both moved to Coventry at the same time, so we rented a house together. During the Second World War, Coventry had been hit hard by the Blitz and was still in the process of being rebuilt in the early seventies. There were amazing new buildings being erected, like Coventry Cathedral, but at the same time there were still streets with craters where the bombs had fallen during the war. I was very hippyish at this time. I wore my hair long, dressed in long flowing skirts and I never wore a bra or a pair of shoes, for that matter. We used to wander around barefoot in Coventry city centre. We weren't given a second glance in London, but in Coventry I definitely drew a few stares.

There was a pub called the Town Wall in the city centre that had been left standing in what was now the car park at the back of the theatre. We became regulars there. I became very involved with the life of the theatre and loved my new group of friends. We were very politically active, we discussed politics, we discussed the world and we wanted this to be reflected in the work that we performed. The political ethos of the company was very much reflected in its day-to-day running. Everyone was paid the same wage, including the director, and it was a cooperative in the truest sense of the word. After a while a large group of us moved into a house together on the main road into the city. It was a large Victorian terrace and there were loads of us living there. It was like being a student again. The camaraderie, the mucking in together, the lack of heating! It was freezing and I would leap out of bed in the morning and charge to the bathroom as quickly as possible to try to avoid getting cold.

It was at this time that my friend Margot Leicester came into my life. Before we married, in my early twenties, Neil and I went to visit his friend in Exeter. Mitch's girlfriend Margot was meant to be there but had gone home to visit her family. After that I heard a lot about this Margot, and from what I heard I would have liked to have met her but never got the chance.

Five years later, when Margot and I first got to know one another, we were out for Sunday lunch one day and it struck me to ask her, 'You didn't go to university in Exeter, did you, and had a boyfriend called Mitch?'

Margot's mouth dropped open. 'You're *that* Sue?'

'And you're *that* Margot?'

What a coincidence! Margot and I became great friends, like the sisters that we never had. We are still incredibly close to this day.

I think that I was at my most politically active at this time. Ted Heath was the prime minister and we were heading towards the time of the three-day week. Looking back, things were very austere at that time. The country was gripped by uncertainty. Unemployment and inflation were high; strikes were weekly. There was a real feeling that the government had no idea what it was like for normal, working people to make ends meet. Sounds familiar, doesn't it? But I think that there seemed to be even less hope for the future then than there is now. Demonstrations were commonplace and I would take part readily. I have always been a big believer in giving a voice to those who do not have one.

Throughout my time as an actress I have been a member of Equity but in the seventies and eighties I was very active in the movement. We would make the journey to the AGM every year in London and in the earlier years it was a family affair with a real air of chaos about it. People would bring their children and their animals. The playwright David Holman would bring his dog Billybags with him, who would trot across the seats and plonk himself down in the lap of the first person he took a shine to. These meetings were a time to catch up with old friends, to spot famous people and generally have a gossip. But as the years progressed, the divides within Equity became more and more pronounced and the meetings more passionate. We wanted change.

The situation at the time was a ridiculous catch-22 for new actors. In order to work as an actor you needed an Equity card, in order to gain an Equity card you needed to prove you had worked as an actor. So for anyone wanting to get into the business there were hoops to be jumped through that to me seemed so unnecessary. Young people had to go off and perform in pubs and clubs, anywhere, just to show they had done something and then they could begin the slow process to being deemed worthy of an Equity card.

I was very passionate about Equity, and still am. I feel that there has to be a union that will step in to represent actors if they are being unfairly treated at work and in pay. However, this wish for change had us labelled as 'Reds under the bed'. Equity was a professional union – more of an association that protected the current members' interests – and most of the old guard wanted to keep it that way. I, and many of the younger actors coming through at the time, wanted Equity to change to form a branch and delegate structure. This would mean that more power would be given to people in the region where they lived and they would have a representative to whom they could go to air any grievances. Vanessa Redgrave often spoke on this issue and at one AGM she stood up to speak. A whisper travelled through the auditorium. Then, as she spoke passionately about the need for change, a chant began: 'Red Queen, Red Queen, Red Queen…' It became louder and louder, people were heckling her, but she remained composed and finished what she had to say. It was quite barbaric to witness, these so-called 'professionals' giving someone such a hard time for voicing her opinion.

Seated behind me on this occasion was a lady who was smartly dressed with a pillbox hat on. She had brought her knitting to keep her occupied. Her friend was sitting next to her, rummaging in a bag of boiled sweets. If you imagine Les Dawson and Roy Barraclough as Cissie and Ada then you wouldn't be far wrong. The woman who was knitting leaned over, her needles still clacking together, and said to her friend, 'They go on these package holidays to Russia and come back with their heads full of these ideas.'

'You're right,' her friend said in agreement before popping another sweet in her mouth. 'And the food's not great there either.'

I did sit on Equity council for a time. I was alongside Kenneth Williams and I enjoyed his company immensely. He was wildly funny and indiscreet and had something to say about everyone. Politically we were poles apart but that didn't seem to matter. He was a real gentleman and I looked forward to the time I got to spend with him.

We never did achieve the branch and delegate structure, and the power of Equity has been greatly diluted since it is no longer a requirement to be a member in order to act. I still encourage young people who are new to the profession to join because if things go wrong and they are treated badly in a job, Equity will step in and fight their corner.

*

One of the stand-out plays we performed at Coventry Belgrade was about Craig and Bentley, which we would use for older children. It is the true story that has since been made into a film about Derek Bentley, a young man with learning difficulties, who was hanged for his part in the murder of a policeman after an attempted robbery went badly wrong. He was famously claimed to have told Christopher Craig to 'Let him have it'. Bentley was in police custody as his friend fired on the police, shooting dead a police constable.

The case was so controversial because all evidence pointed to the fact that Bentley had nothing to do with the shooting of the policeman; it was his friend who had led him there and who had murdered the officer. Also, the fact that a young man with the mental age of eleven was allowed to be hanged begged many questions. It was quite a controversial piece to bring into schools, but we always checked with teachers that they were happy for us to come and perform and workshop afterwards.

There was one lad who was deeply affected by the story of Craig and Bentley. After the workshop he was waiting for us and wanted to come back to the theatre to discuss what had happened. He really thought that there had been a miscarriage of justice and couldn't believe that it had happened in fairly recent times. A few days later he came back to see us, his mind completely changed. 'I've been talking to my dad,' he said, 'and he's in the army. He should have definitely hanged.' He said that his mind was made up. I thought the turnaround in this thoughtful young man was very sad. We were all living and breathing politics at the time. We wanted our group to reflect the world in which we lived. It was very important to us to challenge the status quo and get children thinking. On some occasions the teacher would say that they didn't necessarily agree with what we said, but that the work was always stimulating and thought-provoking and worked in tandem with the curriculum.

We did, however, come in for criticism from the press for being the 'Reds under the bed'. The idea that we were going into schools with communist rhetoric was just preposterous. We were politically minded educational practitioners for sure, but we weren't spreading some sort of ultra-left-wing thinking. We just wanted to introduce stories to children and allow them to think for themselves, to give a fresh perspective to age-old tales. The head teachers in Coventry stood up for us in the face of this accusation, backing our methods and what we brought to their pupils. It was great to have the support from the schools, because we genuinely believed we were doing good, important work with young people.

One other production that we produced and performed was the Rare Earth trilogy. I was working with Maggie Steed, Mervyn Watson and Clive Russell. There were two plays written by David Holman and a follow-up workshop. They were all about the environment long before we knew anything about the ozone layer or the polar ice caps melting.

The first play was about the way that Native Americans were in touch with and respectful of the earth and how the West wasn't. The second was called *Minamata*, named after the small city where a local mercury factory tipped raw waste into the lake where the town's population drew their water supply. It was a true story and very powerful. It was performed using the Japanese Noh theatre style, using masks and mime.

First the wildlife began to die, and then children began to be born with deformities or died from drinking the water. The factory denied any wrongdoing. Lawyers got involved and it looked like the local people would have to bow to the financial prowess of the factory. However, someone in the local community realised that if they bought shares in the factory they could attend the shareholders meeting. They did just that, bringing with them a bucket of water from the lake. They confronted the board and stated that if the water was so safe then they should drink it. They closed the meeting and they were forced to close the factory.

The people of this town overcame the might of the mercury producer. It was a very powerful piece of theatre and has been performed many times since. Theatrically it was very simple. We tried to get the essence of the Japanese people from how with such dignity they refused to accept what was happening to them. It was extraordinary that these people lobbied this huge factory. The play also shows a little girl deteriorate after she ate fish from the lake. Children, as children are, were quite pragmatic audience members. They got it totally, but the most distressed people watching were the teachers weeping in the corner.

Throughout my time in TIE I heard the objection that such complex and emotional issues shouldn't be presented to children. But I think that we should not underestimate their emotional and intellectual capacity.

I still meet people, now in their forties, who remember us visiting their school in Coventry and the positive impact it had. Only a few weeks ago I heard of one girl who saw us and attributes this visit to her going on to join the Coventry Belgrade youth theatre and then went on to be a performer and actress herself.

*

When I first saw Coventry Belgrade perform back at the TIE conference, the director had given a talk when the demonstration was over. He was extremely charismatic and I thought he looked a little like Che Guevara. A few nights later I went out for dinner with our group, and who should be in the restaurant but this handsome director. That evening we spoke, and I have to say from that moment I was smitten. He was funny and witty and utterly charming, and offered me the place with Coventry TIE.

If I'm honest I never thought I had a chance with him but once I moved cities Dave and I began to get to know one another and we started a relationship. I fell hook, line and sinker for him and for the following four years we had a blissful time together. Dave was very exciting and driven by both the theatre and politics. I found him interesting and challenging but also great fun to be around.

One of Dave's hobbies was restoring old cars. He already had a 1933 Morris Minor sports car with a split windscreen, which he thought was the bee's knees. But then he bought a newer 1950s Morris Minor for eight pounds. We had a lot of fun hand-painting it and Dave bought an engine and gearbox from a scrapyard.

Once the car was in working order, we decided to take ourselves to Devon. We managed to get all the way to Devon from Coventry and were rather pleased with the capabilities of our new car. As we headed back home, and were less than an hour from Coventry, the car began spluttering. 'What's that?' Dave asked, pulling on the wheel to keep us driving in a straight line.

'I've no idea,' I said, looking out of the windscreen over

the bonnet to see if smoke was about to come billowing out.

The car shuddered to a halt at the side of a country road. 'It'll be that engine,' I said, 'I knew we shouldn't have got it from the scrapyard. They saw us coming.'

Dave popped the bonnet open. He spent a few moments pulling at wires and looking at the engine, then he pulled his head out and said, 'It's the fan belt.'

'That doesn't sound great,' I said, slumping down at the side of the road, sure that we were going to have to leave our pride and joy on the verge and thumb a lift to a garage.

'It's fixable. Give us your tights, Sue,' he said, holding out his hand.

'My tights?' I said. I had on a lovely pair of brand-new tights, fresh out of the packet that morning, and he wanted me to hand them over for a makeshift fan belt?

'Tights,' Dave said, giving me a wry look.

I huffed and puffed but eventually handed over my tights. I was glad I did, as my faithful hosiery got us home to Coventry!

There was a pet shop not too far from the garage which Dave used when doing up his cars. I had been to see Dave one day when I walked past and in the window were some beautiful, tiny little puppies. They were German Shepherd/Collie cross. I fell in love as I looked through the window and immediately went inside and bought one. She was so tiny and adorable that I put her inside my coat to protect her from the outside world. I then caught the bus to the garage to show Dave my new acquisition. On the way there she threw up all over me!

'Dave, I've got something to show you,' I said when I arrived at the garage, taking this tiny bundle out from my coat.

Dave immediately took the little puppy from me and she nestled in his hands, her big brown eyes looking up at him. 'She's gorgeous,' he agreed.

We decided that we should call her Woodbine, as there was a joke that someone had told Dave about a dog called Woodbine and people would ask if they could take it out for a drag. We quite liked that, so the name and the joke stuck.

A few weeks later Dave came home with another bundle. While he was at the theatre he had seen a little dog in the yard and watched as a caretaker kicked the poor little thing. Dave had gone berserk and asked this man what he thought he was doing to this poor, defenceless little animal. He had picked the dog up and taken it there and then, and that was how we came to have Bugswart, or Bugsy for short. Bugsy had a tail that curled tightly round and she was a real Heinz 57, a mixture of every breed going, and maybe a little bit of pig thrown in. We felt like a real family, and in March 1973 Dave and I married.

We would go and visit his friends John and Dot who lived in a place called Whitworth on the outskirts of Rochdale. Their cottage backed on to a nature reserve and was the most idyllic place, ideal for walking Bugsy and Woody. I became good friends with Dot.

One weekend they called to say that they had spotted a house in the area that would be perfect for us so the next weekend we went up and fell for it. We put in an offer and when it was accepted I was thrilled. A few months later I was offered a job at Bolton Octagon TIE. I had had a great three years in Coventry, but I decided that it was the perfect time for a change.

I moved up to the house and started to settle in to the new area. Dave would follow me twelve months later when he formed a theatre group in the north.

*

When I began work at the Octagon, the first play we performed was on the rise of fascism. They'd had a request from a headmaster in the area because he was concerned about the children in his school being recruited by the National Front. We decided that if we were going to do this play justice we needed to see just how the National Front operated. So I went along with another member of the theatre.

I dressed in a twinset and pearls – a far cry from my usual dungarees – so that I looked respectable and fitted in with the crowd. The police were guarding the event and we were ushered in and told to take a seat. Someone was handing out leaflets with a crude copy of the progression of man from ape. But it had been adapted so that it was about brain size, and claiming to demonstrate that someone from the West Indies had a brain the size of a chimp. I was outraged.

The meeting got going and I've never heard such a load of claptrap in my life. But everyone in that room seemed to be in such agreement at this propaganda and racism. In the end I got so angry I shouted something out, I was very emotional. There was unrest in the room at my comments and a policeman came over and said to me, 'For your own good I think you ought to leave.'

The sheer one-sided bitterness in that room really disappointed me. After that we were galvanised and felt that we really had to do a play that addressed this scape-goating that was going on in the community. We devised a play called *Non Passeran*, which means 'none shall pass' and came from the Spanish Civil War. One of my roles was as a young Jewish violinist who had been forced to play at the gates of the gas chambers at Auschwitz. Mike Kay – who would go on to play a big part in my life along with his wife Veron – played a young Jewish boxer. It was a play that taught about the dangers of complacency against extremism and one that I think is as relevant today as it was in the seventies.

*

As is happening today, Bolton Octagon was soon affected by governmental cuts. We lost our LEA grant and some of us began to wonder if we might be better setting up on our own. We started looking at places where we could house our new venture, should it ever get off the ground. The Gracie Fields Centre had been built in Rochdale and wasn't overrun with people trying to use it, so we decided that if we could set up there and prove we could provide educational theatre for the area, we might be able to qualify for a grant to go into schools.

We left the Octagon and threw all our energies into this new project. We called ourselves M6 because we knew that this venture would involve a lot of touring and that we'd be spending a lot of time on the M6 motorway. We worked in Manchester, London, Bolton and Rochdale. All over the place. We revived *Pow Wow*, which proved as popular as ever. We did a lot of stuff for schools for children with severe learning difficulties. At the time they were called severely subnormal schools – hard to believe now, I know! At one of these schools Maggie Steed was dressed as a clown. The aim was to get the children to teach the clown how to walk and talk. Maggie wasn't allowed to do anything that wasn't a direct instruction from the children. Unfortunately, there was a hole in the crotch of Maggie's costume which one little boy discovered and began working his finger into it. On that day, for the first time, the clown quite rightly stepped out of character and cried, 'Help!'

I was with M6 for about three years. But the company is still around and keeps on going from strength to strength. It has been run wonderfully for over thirty years by Dot, the friend who found me the house in Whitworth. It is one of the most innovative TIE companies in the country, always pushing boundaries, always coming up with fresh ideas. Two generations of children have now benefitted from the work of M6 and that is a credit to Dot and all of her team's hard work.

Chapter Eight

THERE'S AN OLD Native American saying: 'A child is an arrow from the bow. You let them go, you let them go free.' And that is how I have always felt about my son Joel. I may have brought him into the world but he is his own person with his own thoughts and feelings and I hope that I have always respected that.

I was living in Rochdale and working at M6 Theatre Company when I found out that I was pregnant with Joel. It was late 1978, and I was with Dot when I did the pregnancy test. I remember seeing the little blue line and knowing that my life was about to change. At the time my marriage wasn't as perfect as it had been, but I had a very real sense that my biological clock was ticking and that I really wanted to be a mother. Whatever happened, I would make it work. When it hit home that I really was pregnant I was scared to death and delighted in equal measure.

I tried to keep my pregnancy quiet at first. But I was working with Andy Hay and Les Smith, the resident writer at M6, on some pieces of theatre aimed at secondary school children. I had to keep going to the loo and kept falling asleep in meetings. Eventually I decided it was time to tell them.

Taking a big breath, I announced delightedly, 'I'm pregnant!'

'We kind of guessed,' Andy said, laughing.

I suppose the falling asleep on the table was a slight giveaway.

I felt sick for the first three months with terrible nausea that saw me crawling to my bed whenever I could. I'm sure the notion of morning sickness is a myth; I might have been able to manage if it had just confined itself to the hours before midday. Everyone kept telling me, 'After three months it will just go,' and amazingly they were right, overnight I felt fantastic. After that I just loved being pregnant. I bloomed and had a really lovely pregnancy. I understand why some women become addicted to having babies. I think I could have gone on to have several pregnancies if life had turned out differently.

I had been in the pub the evening before Joel was born when I felt a dull ache. My friend Dave Swap was there and we were talking about the fact that there would be a baby here any time soon. 'Well, I hope it doesn't have your feet, Sue,' he said.

'What's wrong with my feet?' I asked indignantly.

'What's right with your feet?' Dave said, laughing.

That night I went home and watched Alfred Hitchcock's

The Birds, which isn't the most relaxing of films, and then I tried to sleep but the ache continued and got worse. This was it.

'I think the baby's coming,' I told my husband Dave, and he grabbed his coat, bundled me in the car and we made our way to the hospital. As I clung to the door handle and tried to breathe through my contractions, we came to a roundabout where a police car was parked in the middle of it. Dave put his foot down and hared around the roundabout, not once, but twice. 'What are you doing?' I shouted.

'I want him to follow me,' he said, 'and when he asks why I'm driving like a lunatic, I'll say, "My wife's in labour"!'

I think the look on my face made him realise that he might have to do without the police escort and just get me to the hospital. Having my husband there made him quite the Renaissance man at the time, I suppose.

When the gas and air was wheeled out, no sooner had I had a go than, playing the joker, he had the tube in his mouth, breathing in deeply. He seemed very taken with it and every time the midwife's back was turned he was on it, high as a kite. I hardly got a look in.

I got my own back. When a nurse turned up with Dave's breakfast, I took one look and threw up all over it!

Other than that, the labour was an amazing experience. I zoned out of everything that was going on around me, breathing slowly and deeply. When Joel popped out into the world and was handed to me, I just had this overwhelming rush of love for him. I was smitten. But the first question I asked was, 'Are his feet all right?' Never mind is he healthy but *are his feet all right?*

The midwife was very surprised at how quickly he had arrived, considering he was my first. 'If you have another one, once you get to nine months make sure you don't cough,' she said with a smile, handing me a cup of tea. No cup of tea tastes as good as the one after labour. I had the shakes, but I was determined to drink it.

'Wait there,' the midwife said, as if it was likely that I would run off down the corridor. She came back a few minutes later with a sippy cup designed for a toddler, full of the precious brew.

For me, having a child felt like I was partaking in the circle of life. Nature takes over your body. All the changes to your body are out of your control. I became very aware of life and death and the order of things, and gained a little understanding of nature's way and what we are all part of. The whole thing had been such a wonderful experience.

It wasn't to last, though. I needed stitches and rather than sending an experienced doctor I'm sure they sent in a child that they'd found on work experience. As Bet Lynch once famously said, 'I've got tights older than him.' And I seem to recall he was dressed like a fisher-man. But what do you say in those circumstances, when you're lying there, vulnerable, legs akimbo: 'Sorry, but do you mind getting me someone who can shave and isn't off to get his first catch of the day after this?'

Being stitched up was the most painful experience I had ever been through. Far more painful than the birth. I started screaming and Dave came running in. I honestly think he thought I must be having twins. Afterwards I was very angry. Why hadn't they anaesthetised me? I felt violated and that my wonderful experience had been marred by this one person. The following day a midwife came to check me. I was telling her of the terrible experience I had had. She took one look at the fisherman's handiwork and said, 'No wonder it hurt, he's sewn through one of the piles!' I wanted to patrol the corridors and find him to inflict the same torture he'd inflicted on me.

After the birth and once the throbbing from the pile incident subsided I slept, as in those days the midwife would take the baby away to the nursery to give the mum some rest. When I awoke I walked down to the nursery to see my lovely little boy, still not believing that it was real – the idea of me, a mum! I walked into the room and all of the babies were lined up in little cots. Joel began to cry and I knew straight away that it was him. There was an immediate surge of milk into my breasts; it was the strangest thing to experience for the first time, that my body knew my baby, out of all the babies in the room.

One thing having a child does is it makes you look outside yourself. It stops you from obsessing over your own problems and focuses you on this other little being who is relying on you for everything. And no one can make you understand the love that you feel for your child. I still find it quite overwhelming.

I don't think they do this in hospital any more, but when I had Joel we had to attend a class to show us how to bathe our new baby. It seemed that most of us were in the same boat on my ward, all new mums who didn't know how to bathe a tiny child correctly. So the midwife set to showing us what to do. She took Joel and soaped him and handed him back to me. I couldn't hold him; I was terrified of him slipping out of my hands. The midwife took him back and said, 'Right then, we'll try you with a Ribena bottle.' She soaped up the bottle and handed it to me. I followed her instructions to the letter and felt very pleased with myself.

I came away knowing exactly how to wash a bottle of pop but none the wiser about how to bathe a baby. It was only afterwards when a friend said that I didn't have to be so regimented and there wasn't an exact way to bathe a child that I realised I could relax and just dunk him in the bath without following fifty separate instructions.

I was on the ward for a few days after having Joel; there wasn't the rush to get you home that there seems to be nowadays. In the bed opposite me was an Asian lady who obviously hadn't been in the country long and understood no English. When she came back from having her child she was in a terrible state, crying and wailing. I thought that something must have happened to her baby. The nurses ran around to see if they could find someone who spoke her language. Eventually, they came back with a doctor who could communicate with her. It turned out that after this woman's baby had been born she saw the afterbirth and thought that it was her soul. She was absolutely terrified. The doctor explained to her exactly what the afterbirth was and left this woman a little more reassured. I did feel very sorry for her, so scared and miles away from her family in this strange town.

On the day I was allowed out of hospital with Joel my parents came to get me. We got back to the house and I wanted my mother and father to stay with me and show me what to do! They stayed for a little while, but of course I had to face the world as a mum and just get on with it. That said, it was lovely to see my parents with Joel. They loved this new baby so much. My dad was so taken with his new grandson. At first he struggled to hold him as he was so small – I think he thought he might break him – but as he got a little bigger and filled out my dad became more confident in picking him up.

It was shortly after I had Joel that my marriage to Dave ended. We had been trying to hold it together but things had been going wrong for some time. I wanted it to work, for us to be a family unit, but I had to admit that we weren't going to be together and quickly adjust to life as a single mother. Because the nature of our work meant that we spent a lot of time apart, I didn't find him not being there all the time particularly strange at first and, anyway, I had a baby to look after. But these things catch up on you and I soon missed him, and started to wonder what had gone wrong and blame myself for the breakdown of our marriage.

I really wanted to be a brilliant mum. I hoped that I would be able to breeze it but anyone who's ever had a child will tell you (and if they don't they're lying!) that it's hard work at first. Back then everyone used towelling nappies, so as well as the sleepless nights, the fretful days and the sheer responsibility of having a child, there was also the relentless washing of bloody nappies! One day I was at the sink, dragging nappies out of the ammonia bucket they'd been soaking in, when I suddenly burst into tears. I remember thinking very clearly, 'I can't do this, I'm going to kill him or drop him or hurt him.' I was on my own and I was really beginning to feel it. I felt so vulnerable and lonely.

I wouldn't let anyone smoke in the house – this is the norm now, but at the time everyone smoked willy-nilly. I would also have the heating on and it was paralysingly hot. One day I called Cathy, a retired midwife friend of mine, because I was worried to death about a rash that Joel had.

'Has he got a temperature?' she asked calmly.

'Well, yes, he's hot,' I said, looking at Joel sweltering in his cot.

'Is he lethargic? Is he responding to your voice?' Cathy

was being the voice of reason in response to my near hysteria.

'Joel!' I said gently. 'Joel!'

His face was red and hot and he looked totally fed up but he recognised my voice.

'Yes, yes he is, but he's covered in this rash and lobster red. I don't know what to do, Cathy,' I said, panicking. 'I think at this rate I'll have to take him to the hospital.'

There was a pause on the other end of the phone then Cathy asked, 'Sue, have you got the windows shut?'

'Yes,' I answered.

'And the heating?'

'That's on too.'

'And is he in his cot?'

'Yes, all tucked in,' I said.

'Sue, it's the middle of summer, the sun's cracking the flags, you don't need to take him to the hospital, you just need to cool him down!'

Poor Joel was dressed for an arctic winter, but it was the only way I knew. When we'd been in hospital the wards had been boiling hot and we would be chastised if we so much as went near a window to open it. I unswaddled my poor boy and not very surprisingly his rash went within the hour.

I was forever putting Joel in the car and rushing him to the doctor's. I'm sure the doctor's receptionist used to peek through the blinds and think, 'Here comes that bloody woman again.'

Andy Hay, one of my dearest friends, was a lodger in the house at the time and my friends Dot and Margot were nearby and I could talk to or ask them for help. Everybody was so supportive and my friends and family really got me through that difficult time. Life began to get back on an even keel.

Another thing that got me through, believe it or not, was the delivery of second-hand twin tub that my parents had bought me. I was finally freed from the nappy drudgery. Not long afterwards I borrowed ninety quid off my mother and bought a washing machine – I thought all my birthdays had come at once when that arrived! It was so joyful as, unlike the twin tub which needed constant supervision, the washing machine could be loaded and left. The wonders of modern technology! I could now go for a nap when Joel slept.

The best advice I got at the time, and that I pass on to any new mums, is sleep when the baby sleeps. Let everything else go and hang. Being constantly tired just exacerbates everything else that you have to deal with as a new mum. Lack of sleep made me feel weepy and despondent but as soon as I had forty winks I was ready to take on the world again. Although I felt down and unable to cope at times, I feel blessed that I was spared the curse of post-natal depression. Having suffered from depression I might well have been predisposed to it, but the black dog stayed away at this time in my life.

I had to go back to work after seven weeks. At the

time, statutory maternity leave was only about three months and I'd used some of it up before I had Joel. I started to get into a panic, as I hadn't made any arrangements for what I was going to do when I returned to work. It had never occurred to me to sign on the dole, and while Dave was generous I didn't want to rely on him for money now that we had split up. Anyway, I have always felt that if I'm capable of working, then I should.

It was my friend Clive Russell – an actor I'd met through Bolton Octagon – who told me straight that I didn't have a choice, I had to get back to work and I needed to sort out some childcare, not just hope that some would fall from the sky. Although funnily enough once my decision to get back to work was made it did feel like my childcare prayers were quickly answered.

One of the actors who was in the M6 Theatre Company said that his wife would be able to look after Joel. She could come to our house in the morning to take over and then I could come home at lunchtime to breast-feed and then return to work. The guilt of leaving Joel at such a young age was somewhat tempered by the trust I had for this lady. I knew that he would be well cared for.

At night I found it hard being on my own. I didn't have anyone to help me with the day-to-day routine: sharing the load while I dealt with working full-time, sleepless nights and breastfeeding...well, they have a term for it now: 'breastfeeding on demand', my term for it was 'relentless'. I remember Veron thinking she was being helpful saying,

'He should be sleeping right through by now,' when Joel was about six months old because her daughter Gemma was sleeping through beautifully. Everyone was chipping in with their 'helpful' advice. I knew what he *should* be doing, he just wasn't doing it! In fact, the first time that Joel slept through for more than five hours I woke him up as I was so worried by the anomaly.

My parents were really helpful throughout this time. They used to come over and clean the house, but my mother being my mother didn't stop at putting the vac round. I'd come home and the entire house would be rearranged. Tables, chairs, beds. When I objected, she looked at me like I was totally ungrateful and said, 'Well, it all looked wrong.'

A few months later the woman who was looking after Joel got pregnant so I was stuck again, but my mother and father stepped in. I had weaned Joel by this time so they used to take him to their house in Warrington, where they'd moved after I left home, and I used to absolutely hate it when he stayed there overnight. I would come home from work to a babyless house and feel bereft. But we established a little routine. My parents would take him off, I'd weep, my mum would tell me to stop fussing and I'd go to work.

I did try him at a babyminder's in Rochdale but he hated it – crying when I left and as soon as he saw me again – so it was back to my parents once more. I have to say that my mum and dad were always fantastic with

Joel, they had such energy for him and there is no way I could have brought him up and gone back to work without them. This for me is testimony to the fact that life just isn't black and white. On the whole, my relationship with my mother wasn't what I would have wanted it to be, I would have liked to be closer, for her to have been more loving. But there were times when she really engaged with me and where I was at. I suppose it was when it was to do with family. Anything outside of our family frightened her, but when dealing with her own she was a force to be reckoned with.

So I kept working and my parents looked after Joel. On his first birthday I was there in the morning but in the afternoon I had to travel to London with M6. It was then that Joel walked for the first time. I hated the fact that I wasn't there, I still do.

Eventually, the amount of time that I was spending away from Joel wore me down. There were times when I was rehearsing and performing and practically a week would go by and I hadn't seen him. I remember working at the Contact Theatre in Manchester and I would try to leave Joel in the morning and he would cling to me. The whole situation had become too much and I needed to address it.

I realised I was again at a juncture, of the same significance as when I decided I had to pursue acting in Liverpool. It required a leap of faith. So I took a two-pronged attack. I made enquiries to see if I might be accepted on a teaching course, but I also applied to agencies to try to find an agent who would represent me for TV and radio work. I was lucky enough to find an agent who would take me on.

Chapter Nine

I HAD BEEN with my agent in Manchester only a short time when she put me up for a role in *Coronation Street* as Mrs Chadwick, the bookie's wife. I got the part and was absolutely thrilled to be given the opportunity to perform in this great British institution.

Nothing prepared me though for actually walking on that set. The street itself looks smaller in real life than you might expect but it is unmistakably Coronation Street. The new houses had yet to be built at the time, and the extra set of the café and the butcher's wasn't there either. It was just the Rovers Return, the row of terraces, the cobbles and the corner shop.

Meeting the actors who played the characters I had watched for years was an experience. I had been an actor for years myself and I knew I should be calm and collected but there was something so iconic about some of those characters that I was as giddy as a kipper.

I was washing my hands in the ladies' toilet at Granada when Doris Speed who played Annie Walker came in. I stopped in my tracks, face to face with a

National Treasure! She came up to the sinks, nodded to me, and then rummaged in her bag. There was so much that I wanted to say to her but I just managed a strangled, 'Hello.'

She reached in her bag and pulled out a wig, which she placed on the ledge in front of the mirror. Then she took off her hat and fitted the wig over her own hair, transforming into Annie Walker in front of my very eyes. I stood there, still washing my hands, mesmerised. She put her hat in her bag, smiled politely and went on her way. I smiled back, still wringing my hands under the tap. She must have thought I was a compulsive hand washer!

I was then called through to rehearsals where I was just awestruck with everyone I was introduced to. They were all very warm and welcoming, there was none of the cliquishness that you might assume goes on with long-running shows like *Corrie*.

Liz Dawn, who played Vera, put me very much at ease. We would go on to become good friends. Then Pat Phoenix came in and she had this amazing charisma about her, your eyes were just drawn to her. She breezed through the room, chatting with everyone. She'd just come back from some time off and had obviously brought with her an unlined face. She claimed it was her second face-lift, and everyone was commenting on how it suited her. I felt like I'd been let into a little club, privy to all this potentially scurrilous information. Years later I would play Pat Phoenix in a TV biopic of her life together with Tony Booth, the actor and father of Cherie Blair. My mother had a picture of me on the wall dressed as Pat with a pack of Pekinese dogs surrounding me. That she loved that picture was due to her admiration for Pat Phoenix, I'm sure!

A little later I was sitting in the Green Room and Bryan Mosley who played Alf Roberts popped his head round and asked if anyone could play bridge. I went to put my hand up to indicate that I did but I couldn't bring myself to speak up, let alone play – I thought I might let myself down with my nervous shaking hands if I agreed to make up the numbers, so I just stayed put.

I was nervous as hell but I knew that it was a great opportunity so I threw myself into it. Watching my first episode on TV, Andy said that I did well but that my shoulders were up round my ears because I was so tense with nerves. I tried to keep my shoulders where they should be for the rest of my TV career. I was cast in three episodes but a few years later I bumped into the casting director who said that they had wanted to bring me back more permanently but I had already got a job elsewhere.

*

It was 1982 and my agent had put me up for a role in a new drama that was going to be set in Liverpool. The producer Phil Redmond – who had previously created and worked on *Grange Hill* – had bought a cluster of brand-new houses for Mersey Television. Six of these formed what would become Brookside Close and the rest were used for the canteen, the editing suite, production office, make-up and wardrobe. Phil wanted the whole thing to look and feel real to both the viewers and the actors.

There was a government enterprise scheme that had just been introduced at the time that Phil took full advantage of. Employers were encouraged to take unemployed people and train them up, and were given a government grant to do this. Phil Redmond and Mersey TV employed people as heads of department who had worked in TV before with the remit that they would be training up the people under them who hadn't, and therefore were eligible for the grant. Apprenticeships are common practice in most walks of life but they were unheard of as a way of producing a TV drama. At the time Liverpool was beleaguered by unemployment and most of us from the area felt that the city had been cut adrift by the southern-centric Conservative government of the day.

This new drama was an opportunity to show the world that life might be hard in Liverpool but it wasn't all destitution, unemployment and poverty. It was a city like anywhere else, with people moving up and down the social ladder. This was something that hadn't been seen before in popular, long-running drama. Long before the new builds arrived on *Coronation Street*, or Ian Beale had a yuppie apartment in *EastEnders* (which hadn't even started at the time) *Brookside* was to show a cross section of society that was more representative of the streets on which most people in the country lived.

There were people who were trying to improve where they lived, like the Grants who thought all their birthdays had come at once moving into somewhere like Brookside Close. Or upwardly mobile couples like Heather and Roger who saw the close as a stepping stone to bigger and better things. It felt fresh and new and in tune with what was going on in the country at the time. Most notably, the action didn't revolve around a pub.

My first audition took place at the Liverpool Playhouse studios on Matthew Street, where the Cavern had been. It was strange to return to my old stomping ground so many years on for what may or may not be another different adventure. I was invited to sit down and was introduced to Phil Redmond and three other people. It wasn't an audition, I wasn't asked to read any lines. It was more like an interview. I talked at length about my work in TIE and Phil really picked up on my political views and pushed me on them. I was happy to get in the ring with him on social issues and only realised later that he was being contrary because he wanted a reaction, he wanted to see what kind of spark I might be able to bring to a character. I left the studios still not knowing what this project was going to be but liking the energy of Phil so much that I wanted to be part of it.

The second audition was at the set of *Brookside*. It was still only half built. The houses were up but there was no road as yet. I traipsed through the mud to the house that was to become the canteen. I was interviewed by Phil and the other producer Colin McKeown and Chris Clough the director.

I was then called back a third time and this time other auditionees were there. As we were all sitting in reception waiting to be called through to read, a big hairy man came in. Everyone seemed to know him; he was shaking hands with all around and cracking jokes. It was, of course, Ricky Tomlinson. He was in a band that played around Liverpool and people knew him as 'Hobo Rick'. I recognised him from somewhere, and then I realised where from. In 1972 Ricky – who had always been heavily involved in the Labour movement – had gone along to support a strike at a building workers' dispute as a flying picket. He was sentenced to two years after being found guilty of 'conspiracy to intimidate', along-side Des Warren who was sentenced to three years. There was a countrywide demonstration to free the Shrewsbury Two, as they came to be known. I joined it when it reached Coventry where I was living at the time. To think that I marched to free someone who would become my future husband, not once but twice!

Eventually, we were all divided into family groups and asked to improvise. It was a very sparky and exciting process, acting as different family members. We then moved around to audition with other actors to see who fit well together. I went home when we were done and prayed that I would get a role. There had been a real buzz about the new show and I really wanted to be part of it. We were told that the series would initially run for three months and then, if it was popular, a view would be taken by the new channel – Channel 4 – as to whether they would extend the run. To have some regular money coming in, even for three months, would be great.

I spent the next few days biting my nails down to the quick. My friend Veron was staying at my house with her young daughter Gemma.

'Will you sit down?' she said as I paced nervously past her for the umpteenth time.

'I haven't got it,' I said despairing, hovering over the phone. 'They'd have called by now. I've blown it.' I plonked myself down on the settee.

Suddenly, the phone began to ring. I leapt to answer it.

'Hello!' I barked breathlessly.

'Hi, Sue,' my agent said. The pause was agonising. I held my breath, ready for the bad news that you always expect as an actor. But instead I heard, 'You've got it!'

I screamed and dropped the phone, then I picked it back up again, thanking her over and over. This telephone call had just changed my life.

'I've got it!' I shouted at Veron. 'I don't know what it is, but I've got it!'

Veron fell about laughing. 'Well, whatever it is then, let's celebrate.'

We didn't have any alcohol in the house so I went in

search of a shop that would sell me a bottle of champagne, not the easiest thing to procure in Rochdale in 1982. I managed it, though, and Veron and I celebrated in style. As we were toasting my success my agent called back in a flap. 'I'm not meant to have told you!' she said. 'It's meant to be a surprise. Keep it to yourself.'

So the next day all the successful actors were called back on set, put into our prospective families and asked to perform some more improvisations. Everyone was still wondering what their chances were of getting a job while I was trying hard not to pop with excitement. Then Phil Redmond came in, looked at Ricky, me and the kids and said, 'You're our Grant family.' My jaw fell, then I began to jump around with glee, hugging the others, appearing totally shocked; best bit of acting I've ever done! I was to play Sheila Grant and Ricky would be my husband Bobby.

In order to have a speaking role on TV you still had to have an Equity card. Barry Grant was actually meant to be played by Joe McGann. Joe was a member of the musicians' union, but he was refused an Equity card because so many cards had been issued to new young actors for *Brookside*. So Paul Usher was brought in to replace him, and was brilliant in the role.

Having spent years acting in theatre productions I remember getting something of a mental block on what I should be doing. I sat down on Sheila and Bobby's bed and thought, 'How do I act to camera?' Even though I had been acting for years, I felt like a complete novice. When you act on the stage it's very important to be bigger than you are, to project the character to the audience. TV is different. It's more intimate. The camera picks up on everything, so I realised I just had to be as natural as possible. In those first few weeks we learned so quickly because we had so much to get through before the show aired. I love learning, so the fact that all of this was new was thrilling to me. Even now I love to learn new things and I'm still open to new challenges. I think that if you give up learning you give up living, or at least give up the opportunity to be part of the changing world.

*

We had been working on the show for weeks and it felt like a comfortable family bubble. There was me and Ricky, our on-screen kids Paul, Simon O'Brien who played Damon and Shelagh O'Hara, who played Karen. Then there was everyone else in the cast, rehearsing and filming together and then socialising afterwards when we had the chance. It was almost like we weren't filming a real TV show.

Because both the show and the channel it was to be aired on were new, we had no preconceptions of what lay ahead. As the transmission date neared, Channel 4 held a press conference. We were to be the second-ever show on Channel 4 after *Countdown*. The press conference seemed to be a big deal and the fact that we were about to stick our heads above the parapet was beginning to dawn on all of us.

Amanda Burton was also an original cast member of *Brookside*, playing Heather. She and I went into town one day when we had a break from our scenes and found ourselves trying on clothes in a communal changing room, as most ladies' changing rooms were at the time. As we pulled various tops over our heads we began to discuss the fact that there might be a remote possibility that once the show started we might not be able to freely swan around shops without being recognised. After all, you did hear about it happening to people who worked on other series. We quickly dismissed it, as if that sort of thing would happen to us! We didn't grasp the popularity and notoriety that *Brookside* would garner. How could we? No one had any idea how this new channel would fare. We didn't even know if anyone would bother watching, it was all so new it had every chance of being overlooked.

*

The day finally came: 2 November 1982. The cast and crew went to a club in Liverpool. We all stood around, drinks in hand, looking at a big screen that had been erected for the occasion, and then the soon-to-be ubiquitous Channel 4 sign came on, the voice-over guy announced that the new channel was in business, and we all cheered.

There was nothing on between *Countdown*, the first show to air, and *Brookside*, not even adverts, just dead air. So we all sat there nervously with our drinks. When the *Brookside* theme tune began to play I got goose bumps. We all watched ourselves in trepidation – that was us up there! When it ended and we all cheered I felt a huge sense of relief.

I arrived home to pick up Joel, and nervously awaited my parents' verdict. I knew that their opinion would go some way to represent how other people in the country had viewed it.

'We liked it, me and your father, but we didn't like the swearing,' my mother said matter-of-factly.

Nobody liked the swearing. Channel 4 received an avalanche of complaints and the writers had to hastily rewrite the future episodes, while the editors took their scissors to the ones already filmed. All the 'effing and jeff-ing', as my mother would have said, was taken out and more palatable terms were inserted. Words such as 'divvy', a previously north-west colloquialism, were inserted instead of harsher terms of derision, and school kids all over the country adopted them as their words. *Brookside* might have caused controversy on its first outing but it had been bought into across the country and the controversy meant that the show had started with a bang. For the actors on the show, our lives were about to change dramatically.

Chapter Ten

I WAS SO pleased I had taken that leap of faith. When *Brookside* came along it was ideal from my point of view. It was local – based in Liverpool. The show aired twice a week and the hours, although long, were not as long as they had been in theatre. And the money was good.

My parents were well settled into their role as grandparents by now. My mum was absolutely great with Joel. My dad was like a dad as well as a grandad to him and that was a real comfort to me. My mother really relaxed a lot at this time. Probably because I'd finally come home and she was again involved in what I was doing.

They were always happy to have Joel as long as it was to do with work. But if my mother got a whiff of me socialising, then the Iron Curtain would come down and I would be treated to her frosty side, so I tried to keep my going out to a minimum.

When the contracts for *Brookside* were renewed it seemed sensible to buy a house near Mum and Dad's. There was six weeks in between selling the house in

Rochdale and buying my new house in Warrington so me, Joel and Woodbine (Bugsy had gone to live with Dave) moved into Mum's dining room.

I don't know how we survived for six weeks in that room without all throttling one another. My mother would stay up for me coming in, even if I was on a night shoot. I'd come through the door and she'd be bolt upright in the chair, scaring the living daylights out of me. It was like being a teenager again. But once we were in the new house it was comforting to be so close to my parents.

My father's relationship with Joel was very special. Joel called him Gramps and idolised him. They spent so much time together and I used to watch my dad shower Joel with love and affection, always attentive to him, always on hand to answer his questions or show him how to do something. I have pictures of the wonderful vegetable patch that my father, with Joel's help, put down in the garden at the house in Warrington.

I had weekends off, which would be unusual now working on a soap opera, but which was normal at the time. Life settled down for the first time since I'd had Joel and I was very content. I had a great job, a wonderful son and my family nearby.

*

As publicity for the show we started being asked to appear in magazines. It wasn't anything like it is now. I didn't run the risk of a photo taken through a long-lens camera popping up on the front of a magazine with me in a swimsuit, or my lack of make-up scrutinised. It was just the odd *Radio* or *TV Times* appearance and the occasional *Woman's Own*.

Bits of tittle-tattle did surface in the tabloids but nothing too intrusive. That was, until a journalist began sniffing around asking about Dave, my ex-husband. I tried to keep a dignified silence; I didn't want Joel or his father dragged into the papers because of my job. However, one of the papers decided that they really wanted to get to the bottom of the story of why we were no longer together and put an investigative journalist on him. Dave called me in a flap.

He had realised that someone was on to him and had been ducking and diving, trying to avoid them. His friends had been winding him up saying that it must be the bailiffs or the taxman. The journalist finally tracked him down to the university where he was working. Dave was so relieved that it was just someone looking to ask him about our marriage that he went for a drink with him and they had a long chat!

I was mortified, but he reassured me that he just wanted to put the whole thing to bed. Other than that I haven't really been pursued by the tabloids, other than the time they put up a picture of myself and Doreen Sloan in *Brookie* under the headline 'Middle-Aged Sex-bombs'. I was only thirty-eight at the time and was shocked to be called 'middle-aged' – I feel like I've been middle-aged for the past thirty years because of that article!

One of the first times I was recognised was in Kendals in Manchester. I was on the escalators travelling upwards and two women stood at the top, waiting for me to reach them. They were commenting on how I was dressed.

'She doesn't look as good off the telly, does she?' one said, looking me up and down.

'No,' her friend replied, curling up her nose. 'I don't like that suit she's wearing.'

I looked down at the trouser suit I had on. I could feel myself burning with embarrassment. Amazed at their audacity, I concocted exactly what I wanted to say by the time I was level with them. But then I panicked. *I can't say anything*, I thought. *They'll tell people that that woman from* Brookside *was rude to them. They won't mention that they were commenting on me and people will think that I'm obnoxious.* I suddenly didn't know how to behave. I had been thrust into a new world where I wasn't sure of the rules – these women knew me, or at least thought they did. I didn't know them and they were talking about me like I wasn't even there. Before I had been 'on the telly' I would have told them straight, but now I was wondering what on earth I should say. I got to the top and powered past them, casting my eyes to the floor.

'How rude!' one of them said loudly.

I didn't turn around to find out which one. What had she wanted me to do? Stop and pass the time of day after the running commentary I'd just heard on the escalator? I kept my head down and kept walking.

As the show's popularity grew, I became more and more recognisable to people. I found it odd at first that someone would want my autograph or want to chat to me about the show, or get me confused with Sheila Grant. I think if I had gone into acting because I wanted to be famous, as a lot of young people do now, I would have felt differently. But I had been an actress for eighteen years, and this was all new to me. I did on occasion say, 'It's Sue!' after being called Sheila for the fifteenth time that day. But after a while I got used to the fact that I was in people's living rooms twice a week and couldn't expect everyone to remember that I had a name aside from that of the character.

*

Working on *Brookside* really was unlike any other job I've had before or since. My memories of being on the show are of us having such a lot of fun. At first, although it was very exciting, it was also a little hairy as we didn't know if the show would work and also we were all learning as we went along. Once it became clear that *Brookside* was a success we managed to relax a little. This allowed us to not only be more confident in our roles and our performances but also to bond as a team. We were working very long hours, sometimes finishing at one in the morning and then back on set for eight the following day. It felt like we were all in it together and as a result we had a lot of fun both on and off set.

We were always very naughty and would take the rise out of one another, especially when there was a group scene as it would mean that the pressure wasn't on one person in particular.

Poor old Bill Dean who played perennial grump Harry Cross used to come in for a hard time. He had great difficulty remembering what he had to say and I would find him taping pieces of paper with his lines on around the set. Open a cupboard door, there were Bill's lines, back of a toilet door, again his lines, a piece of paper taped to a bush on the close, flapping in the wind: Bill's lines. Ricky and Mickey Starke thought it was great fun to remove them so that the poor man was left doing a fish impression into thin air.

Ricky was always playing practical jokes. One day we had a new make-up girl on set. Ricky, with a very straight face, began to tell her his tale of woe.

'I've been having a shocking time recently, girl.'

The poor girl looked concerned as one does when it looks like someone is about to impart something from the heart.

'They've been giving me murder,' he said, nodding down at his nether regions.

The make-up girl's eye widened in horror, I could tell she was feeling terribly sorry for Ricky but really didn't want any further information.

Then he put his hand down his pants and began to rummage around. Her mouth fell open. 'Honestly, me poor nuts!' he said, pulling his hands out of his pants and producing two walnuts. The poor girl nearly died of embarrassment.

Mickey Starke was always trying to put me off when I was going through an emotional scene. I was once midway through a heartfelt speech outside the Grants' house when I saw the privet moving. I looked over to see Mickey's cheeky grinning face poking out at me. I had to ask for him to be removed from the set so I could finish my lines without laughing.

We soon all settled into our new lives and roles as actors on *Brookside* and began to come to terms with the show's success and the difference to our lives that it was making.

One of the biggest storylines during my time at *Brookside* – which happened a few years in – was when my son in the show Damon was killed. It even got its own spin-off episodes, *Damon and Debbie*, where we followed the two of them to Yorkshire where Damon was tragically stabbed. It was a huge hit and teenage girls all over the country mourned the death of Damon.

The day before the funeral, the Grants gathered around the coffin in their living room with a priest. It was a sad affair because it meant that Simon O'Brien would be leaving the show.

I was the distraught mother at the front, but I had

thought it would be funny to bring Simon along. We hadn't been able to fit him in the coffin, so he hid behind the curtains underneath. As we all stood around the coffin, straight-faced, trying to convey the gravity of the situation, a hand curled out from under the coffin lid and grabbed the priest's leg. The poor guest actor let out an almighty yelp and jumped in the air. We all looked as Simon fell out from beneath the coffin howling with laughter!

The poor priest, I think we nearly gave him a heart attack. He needed a lie down in a dark room after that and I bet he never stood that close to a coffin again.

One day I was introduced to an actress who was being brought in to play Marie Jackson. Her name was Anna Keaveney and she was brilliant in the script read-through. I thought, 'My God she's a proper actress!' To tell the truth, I was a little intimidated.

The Jacksons and the Grants became enemies, rowing over the kids. Barry was having an on–off affair with Marie's sister and all sorts of acrimony ensued. One day it all got out of hand and Sheila and Marie had a fight in the street – hair pulling, fists flying, the lot. As Sheila and Marie grew to hate one another, Anna and I grew closer. She was a great friend.

I was very much learning on the job, things that hadn't been a problem when working in theatre were suddenly evident now that the camera was on me. In one of the early episodes of *Brookside* I remember a director saying to me that I didn't blink much. He didn't tell me whether this was a good or bad thing so I took it to be a bad thing, worrying that I was staring blankly at the camera. After forcing myself to blink my way through a scene the following day he asked me what I was doing. I must have looked like I had something in my eye. It was then that I discovered that not blinking too much on camera is actually a good thing.

One of the great things about working on *Brookside* was working with some of the great writers and directors who have since gone on to be huge talents in their field. One of them was Jimmy McGovern. His writing just seemed to get better and better and we were all excited to see what he had written when we were handed one of his scripts. He loved writing for the Grants and we loved performing his work. I once asked him how he wrote so well for women. He said in typical droll Jimmy McGovern style, 'Eileen tells me.' Eileen being his wife. But then he went on to say that emotions are emotions in everyone and it's how you react to them and deal with them that sets the sexes apart. I thought that was such an interesting observation. He has since gone on to create *Cracker*, *The Street* and *The Accused* and I'm proud to say that I worked with him on *Brookside* and again on *The Street* alongside Jim Broadbent.

Frank Clarke is another writer who springs to mind. Frank went on to write the excellent film *Letter to Brezhnev*. Frank wrote an episode for Karen and Sheila where Sheila's Catholic faith was called into question by her daughter who just believed it was utter hypocrisy. It culminated in Karen throwing a lighter from Lourdes with a picture of the Virgin Mary at Sheila, asking if this was really what her faith was about. I then had to slap Shelagh who played Karen straight across the face. The poor girl. We retook the scene a number of times and her face was red raw and covered in finger marks by the time I had finished.

Whenever there is a slap or a punch on TV it is real, or at least that has always been the case in my experience. I used to wallop Simon and Paul across the heads as if I actually was their mother. There was one episode when Sheila had a night out with her friend in town. We didn't often venture off set but this time the producers thought that the audience should see Sheila and her friend Kathy, played by Noreen Kershaw, leave the confines of the close and head into town. This was to be the culmination of months of acrimony between Sheila and Bobby.

On Sheila's return, Bobby was waiting for her and after an almighty row he went for Sheila, actually hitting her. The director was Ken Horn and he promised me that they would do it in one take. So Ricky flew at me and thumped me in the face. As he did I saw my earring fly out and hit the floor and I knew that if Ken saw this the scene would have to be taken again as the previous scene and the next scene had me wearing an earring and the continuity would be spoiled. My face was really smarting so I thought 'I'm not saying anything!' But someone on production said, 'Sue's earring fell out!' And we had to do it again.

Bobby and Sheila were always having heated and sometimes violent arguments. Ricky would say to me, 'Sorry about that, love, do you want your hair back?' And he'd be standing there with a clump of my hair in his hand.

*

Sheila being raped was perhaps the biggest storyline that I undertook at *Brookside*. I was asked to go and see Phil Redmond. I sat down and he looked at me seriously. 'Sue, we're thinking of doing a storyline where Sheila is raped.'

I felt the hairs on the back of my neck stand on end. 'Right,' I said slowly, trying to gather my thoughts.

'I know it'll be a hard thing to pull off but I think we can make it work. What do you think?'

Until then rape wasn't something that had really been broached on primetime TV. But that wasn't my main concern. I'd never talked to anyone other than close friends about when I had been attacked in my twenties. I thought for a moment; I looked at my hands, feeling nervous, guilty and embarrassed about what I was about to say.

'I think you should know, Phil, that I was attacked when I was younger,' I confessed.

Phil was visibly taken aback.

'And if we're going to do it, I need to make sure it's done with the sensitivity it deserves.'

Phil listened as I told him that if we were to go ahead with the story then I was adamant that we shouldn't just produce a sensationalist piece of television. What we screened had to be representative of what women who had been raped went through. I knew the shame and the trauma that stemmed from such a violation, I wanted to make sure that we treated the subject matter carefully.

We went along to the Rape Crisis centre in Liverpool and heard first-hand some of the awful attacks that these women had suffered. And more often than not they were at the hands of someone they knew. We also witnessed the great work that was carried out by the people who ran the centre. The fact that there was somewhere where women could access support after such a terrible event was a step in the right direction, although then, as still today, rape was a crime with a shockingly low conviction rate.

The day of filming came and I was very nervous. I had carried this anxiety around with me for years and I was about to relive it again. The one thing that bothered me was that the attacker was to come at me from behind, something that was still my biggest fear. We filmed it and I managed to get through the day without losing control and being overcome. It turned out to be a great release for me in the end. Acting and performing a rape scene allowed me to get rid of a lot of fear I had carried around for years. When it was over I had a real sense of relief.

When the episode aired there was a huge response from people who had been through the same thing. We received hundreds of letters from women who wanted to share their own experiences; many of these women had been raped and kept silent about it for years.

It is not often as an actress that you get to perform something that you feel directly affects people. Knowing that when I was attacked there was nowhere I could look and think, 'other people know what I've been through', then I felt that this storyline really reached out to women who had first-hand experience of the horror of rape.

Chapter Eleven

I T WAS DURING my time on *Brookside* that I became
involved with the miners' strike. On 5 March 1984
the Yorkshire miners came out on strike at the
proposed closure of Cortonwood Colliery. This sparked
the national miners' strike.

Throughout the seventies there had been a number of
miners' strikes and we had grown used to power cuts and
everyone making a dash for the candles. In the eighties,
though, when the miners went on strike to protest against
what they saw as the plan to systematically shut down
mines across the country it became a battle of wills:
Margaret Thatcher versus the miners. It seemed that
Thatcher's wish was to smash the miners' unions at all costs
as an example to all other workers' unions. Coal had been
stockpiled so that there would be no power cuts and the
government and the miners fought a bitter war. It always
seemed to me that what Thatcher seemed to forget was that
she wasn't battling a theory. It wasn't just Arthur Scargill or
the power of the unions that she went about destroying; she
decimated communities right across the country.

As the government used more heavy-handed tactics and pitted the police against people from their own communities, support for the miners grew. I was incensed at the way these people were being treated. Ricky had always been heavily involved with the trade unions and he wanted to show his support in any way he could, as did I. So the two of us began to make collections from the cast and crew and take the proceeds to Sutton Manor colliery near St Helens.

From these visits I got to know some of the women whose husbands were striking. I was taken by how strong these women were. It seemed to me that they were the heart of the strike. Without the women making ends meet and holding their families together I felt that the spirit of the miners may have been broken far sooner.

One woman, a lady called Sylvia, told me how she had worked in the kitchens at the colliery. When the miners had gone out on strike she had crossed the picket line every day.

'I worked alongside my sister,' she said. 'I knew in my heart of hearts that we shouldn't be crossing the picket line when our husbands and sons were standing on it. But we kept being told by our union that we were doing the right thing. In those early days, the miners were allowed across the picket line for breakfast and lunch.'

Eventually, she realised that working there was sending out the wrong message and that even though they would have no money coming in she needed to stay away from work. Her husband Ken said, 'We'll turn you away from the picket line today.'

'And it was a huge relief,' she confessed. 'I wanted to show my support, to do what was right.'

So Sylvia set up a social kitchen where the community could meet. It was meeting people like Sylvia that made me realise that these weren't hardened lefties out to score points against the government. They were ordinary people, families like my own, who just wanted the opportunity to earn an honest wage.

The papers soon got wind that Ricky and I were visiting the striking miners and that we had begun to attend meetings and rallies. It didn't bother me that it was public knowledge, I was proud to be involved. I attended a rally in Manchester with Jimmy McGovern. Dennis Skinner, my political hero, was there, and I watched in awe as he walked past me. He muttered something to the person he was with and the only words I could make out were 'Sheila Grant'. Recognition of sorts from my idol! He went on to speak and it was extremely moving; he was an amazing orator and had been a miner himself so knew exactly how the miners were feeling. It was around this time that I met Neil Kinnock and began to attend Labour Party events with him. He was always great company and a fantastic politician. I thought it a great shame that he never got to be prime minister.

The miners' strike continued, growing increasingly bitter by the week. I remember very clearly driving into work at *Brookside* one morning and seeing three vans of police parked on the motorway bridge. The policemen were sitting in the vans, no doubt chatting amiably to one another, but they were parked there because they were prepared to go down to the picket line. The altercations between the police and the miners had become increasingly aggressive and I saw these vans as a malignant presence, waiting to stir up trouble. A lot of policemen were as torn as the miners. They were trying to earn a living and this was the job they were given. But this split families. Men who were police officers and men who were miners from the same family found themselves pitted against one another on the picket line.

Eventually policemen were bussed in from different areas, as feelings were running so high on both sides. I had always been brought up to believe that the police were there to protect us, but at that time I had the sinister feeling that the police were there not to protect the citizens of the country, i.e. the miners, but to maintain the status quo.

The strike was long and hard fought. Eventually the miners were returned to work, those who had work to go back to, and the process of closing down the coal industry in this country was begun. It was a very sad time and there was such an air of defeat among mining communities across the country. But when the miners went back, they did so with their heads held high, displaying a dignity that I feel was never shown by the government of the day.

I had quite high hopes for Margaret Thatcher when she came to power. She was a Conservative and nothing in her political viewpoints chimed with my own, but I naively thought that as a woman she would represent women. She was a mother and a wife and surely she would step up and represent the needs and voices of women? How wrong could I have been?

I think that the lampooning of Margaret Thatcher by *Spitting Image* was very clever and summed her up to a tee. Her puppet was dressed in a pinstripe suit and constantly smoking cigars. Essentially, she was a man! I think many women felt let down by Thatcher. She had entered a man's world and proven herself to have a harder edge than any of her male counterparts.

A few years after the miners' strike, in late 1987, Clause 28 was introduced into the Local Government Bill by the Conservative MP, Dame Jill Knight. It banned 'the promotion of homosexuality' as a 'normal family relationship'. The following May the bill was passed. There was outrage from gay rights campaigners, of which I was one. As far as I was concerned it was regressive policy-making and thinly disguised homophobia. Two members of my extended family were gay, I had lots of gay friends and colleagues and I knew what a struggle it was for people to come out. When I was younger, of course, it had been illegal, so I knew how hard fought the battle for gay rights had been. For a few years it had felt that society was progressing forward in its acceptance of homosexuality but now Clause 28 had been passed in to law, which legitimatised discrimination in my opinion.

I met the actor Michael Cashman, an ardent gay rights campaigner, through this. It is also where I met Ian McKellen. It was Ian's involvement with the fight to abolish Clause 28 that forced him to come out. This was the case for a lot of people, it made them come out and say they were proud to be gay. The very opposite reaction to the one the government were hoping for, I'm sure!

I went along with Michael to a large demonstration in Manchester. I hadn't intended to speak but as I stood at the front it was suddenly noted that I was there and I was hoisted up on to the platform. There I was looking out over this large crowd. 'Bloody hell,' I thought, 'I'd better say something and quick!' The famous speech by Pastor Martin Niemöller came to me:

> First they came for the Jews, but I did not speak out because I wasn't a Jew.
> Then they came for the Communists, but I did not speak out because I wasn't a Communist.
> Then they came for the trade unionists and I did not speak out because I wasn't a trade unionist.
> Then they came for me and there was no one left to speak out for me.

I went on to say that we all had a responsibility to speak out where we saw injustice and that what the government was doing to the gay community was deeply unjust.

The movement to abolish Clause 28 galvanised people. Rather than push people into a corner it made them come out and be proudly gay or support the gay community. Of course, there was a large number of people in the country who agreed with it, who were delighted to have some actual legislation to give legitimacy to their bigotry. It would take a further twelve years for Clause 28 to be abolished by the Labour government in 2000.

I continued to be a supporter of the Labour Party. My aunty Jocelyn used to say, 'You'll vote Conservative when you get older, mark my words!' Well, I can confirm that at the age of sixty-seven I might be slightly disillusioned with party politics but my pen has yet to put a cross beside the blue party.

Chapter Twelve

I T DIDN'T TAKE long before people got wind that 'Sheila Grant' lived in my house. Strangers would come and sit on the wall and stare through the windows, so we'd spend most weekends with the curtains drawn. I took to not answering the door when there was a knock. One weekend, however, I was waiting for a friend, so when a knock came at the door I answered it.

'Sheila Grant?' the woman asked, standing there in all her finery.

'Er, yes...' I stammered.

She turned to her friend and shouted down the path, 'It is her. Told you. Come and have a look.'

Then she turned back to me and said matter-of-factly, 'We just came to have a look at you.'

They both continued to stand, staring at me. I'm not sure what they expected me to do – invite them in and make them tea and talk about our Damon and Barry, perhaps? After what felt like an eternity of me staring at them and them staring at me, my friend rounded the corner.

Seeing these two women hovering in front of the door, who I obviously wasn't inviting into my home, she ushered me inside and said curtly to the women, 'She's very busy at the moment.'

And the two women looked very disappointed to have to cut their day out short.

A couple of weeks later there was a man in my garden late at night staring up at my bedroom window. This might not have had any conncection to Sheila Grant, he could have been more interested in my video recorder. I threw the window open. 'What the bloody hell do you want?' He looked startled and then asked, thinking on his feet, 'Do you know what time it is?' Like I was the speaking clock. I called my neighbours who rang the police.

After this I began to feel quite vulnerable in the house. I think the straw that broke the camel's back was when I threw a party where a lot of the cast and crew from *Brookside* came along. Word soon got out around the area and kids arrived from miles around. Pretty soon the whole thing descended into bedlam. After that I decided that I really needed to move to somewhere where Joel didn't have to put up with all these intrusions. He was five or six at the time and I didn't want his life adversely affected just because his mum was on the telly.

Frank was a close family friend who had bought a property at auction that he was doing up for himself and his family to live in. It was in the middle of an estate and surrounded by trees. Years ago there had been a stately home there called Enfield Hall, with a villa, cottages and stables attached. The hall had since burned down, but Frank had bought what remained, which had all gone to rack and ruin. He set about refurbishing the houses and mentioned that he would sell one to me if I was interested. The house he was talking about was in such disrepair at the time that I couldn't secure a mortgage on it so I tried to put the idea of living there out of my mind.

Months later, Frank told my parents that the house was nearly finished and asked if I'd like to go and take a look. It was perfect. The little area that he'd bought was an oasis from the more modern houses nearby. It had a footpath that led straight through the trees to a brook. It felt calm and peaceful and somewhere Joel and I would be happy to live.

So I bought the house from Frank and went back to my parents' dining room while the building work was completed. This time we had a new dog in tow. Woodbine was still with us but now we also had Ben, a big golden retriever who I'd bought on Joel's sixth birthday.

Shortly before, Joel had been sitting on his bed and I sat next to him and said, 'Do you know what you'd like for your birthday?'

Joel looked at me and with earnestness that only a child can muster said, 'A brother, a sister or a dog.'

I nodded as if I was carefully weighing all three

options up, 'Okay, I'll see what I can do.' As a single mother with two days to go till his birthday, his chances of getting one of the first two of his requests were slim to none, but I was happy to go with the third. So Ben arrived in our lives.

We had had Ben for a few days when Joel came to me one day to say that he couldn't find his socks. I put this down to him not being bothered to look. But then when I went to find a pair in their usual place, they'd gone too. Later, when I took Ben out for a walk, he grunted and strained until he finally passed what on closer inspection turned out to be a knitted poo. He was a sock eater. Paul Usher once looked after him while a friend of his was staying over. His mate had a pair of brand-new Adidas socks that were all the go and quite expensive. Of course, Ben took a fancy to them and by the time the Adidas socks worked their way through Ben's system, his friend wasn't so keen on his new socks any more. He was lucky, Ben was also known to demolish a pair of my knickers from time to time.

Anyway, we moved into the new house in Cinnamon Brow on 23 December 1986. We hadn't unpacked, we put some blinds up and a Christmas tree, made sure the table was in the family kitchen and we were ready to have Christmas there. Poor Joel was devastated to leave the old house and his friends from the street behind. When children love somewhere it's hard for them to imagine that anywhere better will come along. But he soon settled in and quickly grew to love our new home. And because it was quite secluded I didn't find myself with visitors sitting on the wall having a gawp every weekend.

*

My mother hated me being recognised, it fell into the category of Drawing Attention to Myself, something that was on her list of social no-nos. The fact that she deemed my entire career to be Drawing Attention to Myself didn't help either. My aunties, on the other hand, loved it when people stopped to chat with us. We were in Blackpool one day having a pub lunch when a few people spotted me and came over to talk.

'Hello,' said Aunty Jean brightly. 'Are you here on holiday or just for the day?'

My mother was giving Jean an evil glare, which Jean duly ignored.

The ladies informed her that they were there for the weekend and asked us about our trip. Jean was more than happy to tell them about what a lovely day she was having as my mother silently seethed across the table. Eventually, this all became too much for Mum to put up with and she leaned across the table and hissed, 'Stop encouraging them, Jean!'

'Why are you embarrassed?' Jean asked with a dismissive wave. But my mother couldn't answer and instead pursed her lips, as she often did when stuck for something to say.

People would often say to my mother during these type of encounters, 'I bet you're proud of her, aren't you?' She would smile tightly but she would never answer. I think she just wished that I'd get off the telly, stop Drawing Attention to Myself – and by proxy her – and let her get on with her life!

Being on *Brookside* meant that I was given the opportunity to go to events like award ceremonies, and I liked to try and include my mother. But she would often clam up, and seem to not be enjoying herself. The days would sometimes end with her not speaking to me and I'd feel that I'd failed her somehow. I used to get very upset about these occasions; I suppose I was just trying to encourage my mum to enjoy herself and to take advantage of the things that now came our way. But looking back my mother was happiest and most at ease when in the company of her family. Taking her to these dos placed her entirely out of her comfort zone and I can understand now why she wanted to simply go home and have a cup of tea.

That said, she did love it when we were out and my friends made a fuss of her. I took her to York Races and she really was Queen Bee for the day. She was delighted when I asked her for tips, as, along with her brothers and sisters, she was a keen gambler (although they'd say, 'We only play for pennies!') We had a wonderful meal and Mum really enjoyed the day and the attention that she received. She also loved seeing Dean Sullivan who played

Jimmy Corkhill in *Brookside*. He is a great friend of mine and would always make a big fuss of my mother.

He would say to her, 'Look at you, Margaret, eh? Looking as gorgeous as ever.' Mum would always have a twinkle in her eye when Dean was around and I really felt that I could relax when he was there as Mum thought so much of him.

*

It was around this time that my eating demon reared its ugly head again. I had begun a relationship with a lovely man but he was very keen on taking the next step and settling down and having children together. I really liked him but I didn't want this. I wasn't sure I needed a husband with all that that entailed. I was happy with my life with Joel. I found the situation very stressful and it is at times of stress that I now know I begin to over- or under-eat.

There were other things in my life at the time that contributed to me turning my attentions to the rigid control of food. I have never liked seeing myself on-screen and only ever watch myself as a technical exercise to see how I can improve things. But I was on TV all the time now and I became acutely aware of my appearance. Having spent years of chasing my ideal weight – although I honestly don't know if I even knew what that was – I hit upon an idea. I really did think that I'd somehow found the answer to my problems, rather than

I was embarking on an even darker road with my relationship with food. I had some notion in my head about the fact that the Romans had vomitoriums, where they would purge themselves after gorging on food. The Romans were a civilised bunch, I reasoned, so surely they knew what they were doing. What a way to justify something, but I was clutching at straws.

So I began making myself sick. I would eat my lunch, go to the toilet, stick my fingers down my throat and throw up. I'd flush the loo and then return to whatever I had been doing, purged, as if this was part of a perfectly healthy routine.

It became something that I did after every meal. I was triumphant, feeling that I could eat what I wanted and with one simple trip to the toilet and my fingers down my throat I wouldn't put on weight – my dieting prayers answered. I didn't give any thought of what it was doing to my stomach, my gums and my teeth, which began to decay from all of the stomach acid eroding them as it made its way into the toilet bowl. And that's not to mention what it was doing to my mind. I was constantly obsessed with food to the exclusion of everything else, and this went hand in hand with an intense self-loathing.

Looking back at pictures from that time, I look awful. I started to feel exceptionally low, but I never thought about going to the doctor about it. It wasn't something I considered a problem at first, it was just a means to an end. I was getting desperate and knew that I needed help because I simply couldn't stop on my own. I began to eat any old rubbish, shoving it down my neck and then throwing it up again. I was treating myself like a dustbin. It was disgusting. A continuing cycle of gorging and purging.

Anorexia had begun to be talked about in the media at the time but bulimia wasn't really. So I didn't think of it as an illness, I didn't even have a name for it; it was just what I did. It was all so tied up with emotion and the depths of my subconscious that I wasn't sure what I was really dealing with.

After a while, though, I became convinced that it was damaging me. I was utterly horrified with what I was doing to myself but I couldn't stop. I would look in the mirror and cry with shame. I would think to myself *I'm in my early forties, not some silly teenager!* It took me years to confront my fears. It was a conversation with a friend that finally made me realise that I had a problem so out of control that I needed to seek professional help. She admitted that she had been bulimic for a few years and as she spoke I just came out with it. So was I. Just saying it out loud helped me. It gave me some relief from the guilt and the shame. I finally went to the doctor and told him how I had been suffering.

The journey from bulimia back to health was a slow process. I was prescribed antidepressants again and they helped kick-start my recovery and gave me a more positive frame of mind. After that I had to be diligent and honest with myself. I had to acknowledge what triggered the feeling that led me to make myself sick. There were times when I would find myself stood over the toilet bowl and I would have to talk myself around.

When you admit to an eating disorder, it's amazing how many people confess that they been in the same boat as you. I think many women have an unhealthy relationship with food and it's only getting worse as girls are exposed to unrealistic body images from an increasingly early age. I always think that an eating disorder is a particularly cruel form of addiction as the person suffering from it cannot abstain as with alcohol or drugs. You still need to eat. I have had to keep on top of my relationship with food and try to eat healthily and exercise. Bulimia not only eats away at you physically but mentally too and I am glad to say I can look back on it and be thankful that it is something that I don't suffer from now, although I will always be mindful of how and what I eat.

Chapter Thirteen

WHEN I WAS younger my dad used to take me to both football and rugby and on occasion Mum would join us to watch the rugby. St Helens was Dad's rugby team and Warrington was my mother's so there was a good-natured rivalry between them. When I got older I used to also go to watch St Helens with my friend Marj and as a youngster I probably went to more rugby matches than football, but as I got older that was all to change. My dad's football team was Liverpool and football was a huge part of my father's life. I'm very pleased to say that because of his influence it is a huge part of mine.

If my dad was listening to the match indoors, he would perch on the edge of the chair in the sitting room, one ear to the radio. But more often than not I would wander outside to the shed to find him crouched over his radio listening to the football. I would always keep up with Liverpool and where they were in the league but it wasn't until I moved to London in my twenties that I became an avid football fan. Rugby league wasn't something that had travelled as far as London in those days, and there was no local team that might give cause for St Helens to visit, so, needing my sporting fix, I turned to football and Liverpool. Whenever they came down south to play one of the London teams I would go to support them. It was great to have that connection, not only to home but also to my dad.

Although I tried to get to the game as often as I could, being down south meant that more often than not I would only see away games. When I went back to work in the north, and more specifically when I started work on *Brookside*, I began going to see Liverpool religiously.

For me, being a Liverpool fan is as much about the camaraderie and spirit of the club and its supporters as it is about following the team. I love being immersed in the banter that goes on at the match. I think that a lot of this comes from working somewhere that has two teams in one place. When I had worked in the tax office in Liverpool in my teens I had enjoyed the slanging matches that used to go on between the Liverpool and Everton fans. Football is so integral to the city and is woven into the psyche of the people.

Joel was eight when I first took him to Anfield Road. We played Coventry City and lost. He was so disappointed afterwards that I was sure he wouldn't ever want to go again. At Joel's school everyone was into rugby as Warrington is a big rugby league town so, like me, Joel was more enamoured with rugby than football when he was younger. But as he got older he became more and more interested in football and today he is Liverpool's biggest fan.

There were a couple of incidents when Joel was young that made him want to stop going to the away games altogether. One time we played Manchester City at their then ground, Maine Road. We were sitting among the City fans and they began chanting obscenities at me, the stewards had to take us out and put us behind the dugout. Then another time we went to a Manchester United game and I was called a 'Scouse Bitch' by a United fan.

When things like that happen I have always felt that the Liverpool fans protected me, that when we were in the middle of the Kop everything was safe. When I was asked to draw a raffle at Middlesbrough one year there was a resounding 'You Scouse Bastard' being chanted by the home crowd. I thought it was quite amusing if I'm honest, but I was delighted to hear the Liverpool fans who had travelled to the game chanting back, 'There's only one Sue Johnston!'

On the set of *Brookside* there was great banter between the supporters of both sides. Simon O'Brien, who played Damon, came in for particular stick. His character supported Liverpool, but Simon was a life-long Everton fan. So any time he had a line praising Liverpool we'd make him repeat it and get the director to pretend he needed a retake. The poor lad was driven crackers by this constant ribbing of his precious Everton.

In April 1989 I was working on a book and I was very behind deadline. I had been at the Grand National the previous week and had met with a few of the Liverpool players and their wives. I was invited to the upcoming away game; Liverpool were to play Sheffield Wednesday at their home ground Hillsborough. I readily accepted the offer only to be told by the editor of the book that she was getting on a train and coming to see me in order to get me to submit the manuscript in a timely fashion. I had to relinquish my tickets for the game.

It was 15 April, and a beautiful spring day. I'd left the TV on in the house as we worked outside. As the game began I popped my head in to see if there had been an early score. I looked at the TV but couldn't work out what was going on. At the time huge fences had been erected at a number of football grounds and the plan was for them to be installed at all football grounds to prevent pitch invasions. People were scaling the fences and spilling onto the pitch.

Bruce Grobbelaar was waving his arms trying to stop the match. I stood with my hand over my mouth. Had some sort of riot gone on, I wondered. The Heysel disaster, where Liverpool fans had rioted with Juventus supporters resulting in thirty-nine deaths of the Italian side's fans, was only four years before. Now this was happening in front of my eyes. I couldn't believe it. People were penned in behind the fences, desperate to get out to avoid being crushed. Those who could, climbed up the stand and were reaching to the upper stand for help.

I called to my editor and we both watched it unfold. It was a truly terrible day. People were tearing up hoardings to create makeshift stretchers. Fans were being brought out and laid on the pitch; at the time we didn't know that some of them were the bodies of those who had died.

My cousin Bob had gone to the game and of course in those days there were no mobile phones so there was no way of knowing if he was safe. He had to queue up outside someone's house and call to let the family know he was all right.

I drove the editor to the train station later; the radio was on and they played 'You'll Never Walk Alone' and 'Eternal Flame', which was number one at the time but seemed very poignant. In between each song the DJ gave out more information about what was happening in Sheffield. Each time, the death toll had risen and the reports from the ground had become more harrowing. In total, ninety-six people lost their lives and 766 people were injured.

Bob called the following day to say that a service was going to be held in the Liverpool Cathedral for the victims. I picked up Bob and drove to the outskirts of Liverpool city centre and walked into town. The streets were full of people heading in the same direction, heads bowed in silence. It was such a moving experience to see all these people with a common purpose. Once we got to the cathedral we realised we couldn't get near, there were thousands of people outside who had all come with their shared grief.

Knowing that everyone was there to hear the service and that no one wanted to go home until it was finished, priests walked through the crowds holding up transistor radios transmitting the service inside. People were passing their scarves along the crowd to be tied to the railings of the cathedral. An Everton fan standing in front of me passed his scarf forward. It was an extraordinary time for both teams. These rivals were joined in this common bond, a city-wide grief. Team flags were tied between Anfield and Goodison Park, uniting the two clubs. The service came to an end and everyone drifted off, again in silence.

During the week following, the *Sun* newspaper printed a headline stating: 'The Truth'. Underneath was a story saying that Liverpool fans had urinated on the police and had pickpocketed the bodies. It was a disgusting smear on not only the club but the people of Liverpool and their grief. None of this was substantiated. Overnight the *Sun* was virtually outlawed in Liverpool. To this day there is wide disregard for the *Sun* newspaper in the city. Other newspapers didn't fare much better, printing 'tribute' editions with the pictures of those who died as they were being crushed. The whole thing seemed to be handled with an immense lack of sensitivity towards the victims' families by the press.

On one of the days following the tragedy I drove to the ground with John McArdle who played Billy Corkhill in *Brookside* and some of the other cast and crew. We walked through onto the pitch to the most breathtaking scene, the pitch was covered in flowers from the goal to the halfway line. We stood and took it all in. Flowers had been piled on flowers, scarves had been tied to the railings and again there was this terrible silence. There really was a weight of sorrow over the city. As we were walking back off the pitch a steward stopped us and said that there were some relatives here that had asked if we would meet with them. I wasn't sure what I could do in this awful time but I was more than happy to speak with them. I was introduced to a mother whose son had died. She was absolutely desolate with grief. 'You know how it is, Sheila, you've lost a son...' she said to me, referring to what had happened in *Brookside*. She was in a total state of shock. I took her hand and just sat with her letting her say what she needed to say.

The club wrapped its arms around the people involved. It was like a home for those who didn't know where to go with their grief. The players all attended funerals but Kenny Dalglish, who was player-manager at the time, went to every single one. You could see the grief weighing in his face as each funeral passed. I think that this is why Kenny eventually moved away, the whole experience had crushed him. Of course, he is the only person who can really say this for sure. Whether or not that is the reason, he is back now but has always been a hero to the club.

A month later we got through to the final of the FA cup and by serendipity we were to play Everton. Gerry Marsden sang 'You'll Never Walk Alone' and it was the first time I had seen the Everton fans join in, it was extremely moving. Fittingly we went on to win. As the final whistle blew a small part of the crowd ran on to the pitch as the fences had been taken down as a matter of course after Hillsborough. Where I was sitting people began booing and slow clapping this minority of idiots and the sheer force of the sound of the crowd shamed them back onto the terraces. We were glad to win but it was a very subdued celebration.

Soon afterwards details began to emerge that made many fans begin to question how the event had been policed and if it was something that could have been prevented. To this day the families of the ninety-six who died have unanswered questions and feel that justice has never been served. Every year there is a memorial service and every year the names of each person who died is read out and a candle is lit in their memory. It was my privilege to be asked to read a lesson at a service a few years ago.

Outside the ground is a memorial, it has all the names etched in stone and an everlasting flame burns. It is always festooned in flowers and scarves and sometimes when I'm walking into the ground I'll see someone kiss their fingers and touch a name, something that I find very moving every time I witness it. Their loved one's memory lives on.

*

I am immensely proud to be a Liverpool fan and am proud of everyone who supports the club. For me, Joel, and my dad when he was alive, it is more than a football club, it is a way of life.

On *Brookside* I was given the opportunity to do things I would never have been given in ordinary life. One time we were playing in a charity football match that had been organised: *Brookside* Women versus *Grange Hill* Girls at Goodison Park. I would obviously have preferred to play at Anfield, but the idea of being allowed on the pitch of our rivals filled me with an odd feeling of pride. This feeling was soon to evaporate, however, when it became clear that I should always be a spectator and not a player of my beloved football. I was so unfit! We all were. The *Grange Hill* Girls ran rings around us. If I did get chance to hoof the ball anywhere on the pitch I didn't have the energy to go after it. I have to say we weren't taking it particularly seriously as our goalkeeper was Ricky in a wig and false boobs. We crawled off the pitch at the end of the match. I said to Joel afterwards, 'Not many people who can say their mothers played at Goodison Park.' He raised an eyebrow and said, 'Not many people would want to either.'

My most treasured memory relating to my father and Liverpool was having the opportunity to take Dad to Wembley to a cup final. Liverpool were playing Manchester United and the tickets were like gold dust. I had begged and pleaded around the cast and crew of *Brookside* for two tickets to no avail and a few days before the match I had given up all hope.

Then Paul Usher wandered over to me and casually asked, 'Still fancy the match at the weekend, Sue?'

My eyes narrowed, of course I did, but was this a wind-up? I thought he was going to laugh and say 'tough!'

'Yes, why?' I asked tentatively.

'Because I can get you two.'

My jaw dropped. 'Who from? I'll have them!' I said immediately, jumping with excitement. Paul was friends with Craig Johnston who played for Liverpool and later that day Craig dropped the tickets at the set. I called my dad with the news that I knew would make his year: 'Dad, get ready, we're going to Wembley!'

I booked first-class tickets on the train as I wanted to make this a special day for my father. He had his packed lunch with him and we headed off to the final. We got on the tube to Wembley and all the Liverpool fans were singing, 'There's only one Sheila Grant!' which my dad thought was fantastic. When we got to the ground it was such a delight to see Dad walk into that hallowed stadium. We had such a fabulous day together. It was lovely to see him taking in the atmosphere and enjoying himself so much. On the way home on the train Dad realised that opposite us was the legendary footballer Sir Tom Finney sitting with his wife. Tom had been known as the Preston Plumber when he played for Preston North End. Dad began chatting to him and the two whiled away the hours back up north chatting about their shared histories: plumbing and a love of football. It was lovely to see these two men enjoying one another's company; both legends in my eyes. We arrived back home having had a wonderful day together.

The following year we played Everton in the cup final and I asked Dad if he'd like to go. 'No, love,' he said, thinking back to the great day we'd had the previous year, 'I'll go out on that. It was perfect.'

He was right. And I have our shared love of football to thank for having that bond and those special shared moments over the years.

Chapter Fourteen

JOEL WAS ALWAYS such a laid-back boy and as an adult he is one of the most unflappable people I know. He wasn't particularly flustered by any of the hulla-baloo that came with his mum being in *Brookside* when he was younger but as he got older he did begin to become more aware and more embarrassed by it. There were times when we'd go to the local precinct and we'd be practically mobbed. *Brookside* was hugely popular with teenagers, they loved it – and as everyone knows, when teenagers are fans of something they are ardent fans! Girls would scream at me as we went past. Dared by their friends to say something, or so giddy with excitement at seeing someone they recognised from *Brookside*, they would shout the first thing that came into their head. This upset Joel, it scared him and he didn't like the attention that we received. As he got a bit older I found that the same thing was happening when I went to pick him up from school. The kids were starting to recognise me.

Joel went to a junior school nearby, but by the time it came to him moving up to secondary school I was very wary of him going to the local comprehensive. It is such a hard decision to have to make for your child. My parents couldn't understand why he couldn't just go where his friends were going but I felt that he should have a clean break from being known as Sheila Grant's son, somewhere he could just be himself.

I eventually found a school at the other side of town. I took Joel to see it and he liked it. I felt much better knowing that he was happy about the change too, and once there he really enjoyed it. I did on occasion pick him up from his new school, but I would hide around the corner so that he didn't have to have the awkward conversation with his classmates that yes, his mother was in *Brookside*.

*

Brookside had been going from strength to strength, and Ricky and I did two great specials together. One was in the Costa Del Sol in Spain. We were staying in the centre of Benidorm and we got a lot of people following us around as we filmed or when we went out at night. So in the end someone on the production team suggested we hire a villa in the sticks and drive in for filming. It was a beautiful place, surrounded by orange groves. The owner of the villa was extremely kind to us and took us to a restaurant up in the mountains. There was Ricky and me and the director Chris Clough and Ken Horn who was then the cameraman. We sat down, jugs of sangria were placed on the table, and so began a night of eating, drinking and merriment. Ricky was up singing and entertaining everyone and we had a fabulous time. At the end of the night, when we were all fit to burst and sozzled, I reached into my bag to get the kitty and realised I didn't have it. By this time the owner of our villa had gone and we were communicating in our pidgin Spanish. The others couldn't believe I'd left the kitty behind. Ricky pulled the inside of his shorts pockets out to indicate no money. We did the washing-up mime to indicate that that's what we might have to do to go some way to paying for our meal. In the end after a number of 'mañanas' and more pocket pulling from Ricky, we conveyed that we would be back the following day to pay for our meal. We were. And it became our mountain hideaway for the rest of our time there.

Another time Ricky and I went to film Sheila and Bobby on a second honeymoon in Rome. We were perched on the side of the Trevi fountain. The fountain is famous for two things: the scene from Fellini's *La Dolce Vita* and for visitors throwing coins in and making a wish. There were hundreds of coins under the water. Ricky was about to do a big emotional speech to Sheila about what this moment meant to him.

Suddenly Ricky started twitching his head and speaking like a ventriloquist.

I leaned in. 'What?' I asked.

'Them fellas, over there,' he said through gritted teeth.

I turned my head slowly to see two men, very smartly dressed with a carrier bag at their feet. With them they had what could only be a giant magnet, and they were using it to fish in the fountain. They were shoving it in and then trying to surreptitiously flick the coins into the carrier bag. They were stealing the coins! Someone must have alerted the police because they were there in moments and the entrepreneurial thieves fled through the street chased by the Polizia.

*

Brookside was such a great programme to work on but after eight years I began to feel restless. The storylines for Sheila had always been strong and I thought it was fantastic when they decided to send Sheila off to college to get an education. I knew that this would chime with a lot of women of my generation who had brought up their families and were now turning some of their attention to themselves. This storyline, though, drove a wedge between Sheila and Bobby, and in retrospect I think it drove Ricky and me apart at that time too. We both felt that our characters were being changed but we reacted to this in very different ways.

Sheila had an affair with John McArdle's character Billy and then her Catholicism became very extreme. I began to worry that the stories were becoming a little out of character. When Sheila left Bobby and moved in with Billy, and in doing so lost her family, I felt that this development strayed away from who she was.

It was always a real joy to work with John and perform the Billy and Sheila storylines, they were very popular and we even went on *Wogan* when the characters kissed for the first time. However, once they were together and they were accepted as a couple I felt that the storylines began to fall away and Sheila just became a bit of a religious obsessive.

Ricky started to worry about the character of Bobby when he seemed to be shifting away from his working-class roots. Bobby had always been a family man and a trade union man. But when one script asked that Bobby act prudishly about his daughter Karen moving in with her boyfriend, Ricky saw red. Why would someone who had been a left-wing unionist all his life give a monkey's about his daughter moving in with her boyfriend out of wedlock? Sheila, maybe, she was the Catholic, but not Bobby. Ricky began to distance himself from the producers who he felt weren't listening to him and things began to feel awkward on set.

Things came to a head around Christmas time. Phil Redmond would throw a party on Boxing Day every year and invite the cast and crew. This year I went along and Ricky hadn't been invited. Later, he was very upset that I hadn't told him about the party and felt that I had let him down. I just felt that I was in an awkward position: it hadn't been my party to tell him about. He left *Brookside* soon after. If I'm honest, I didn't feel that the character of Sheila was ever really right once Bobby had gone.

*

It was at this time that my friend Andy Hay who was directing at the Octagon Theatre – my old stomping ground in Bolton – contacted me to say that he was developing a play with Jim Cartwright. He said that they thought that John McArdle and I should play the parts if there was any chance we could get a sabbatical from *Brookside*. This definitely wasn't the done thing, but John and I decided that we would ask.

The idea of doing something different if only for a little while really appealed to me. Phil Redmond agreed to give us two months off and so John and I began workshopping the play with Jim and Andy and the result was *Two*. *Two* is set in a pub and the central characters are the landlord and landlady. As the play progresses, a succession of other couples come in and we are given an insight into their lives as well. The play was very simple with all of the characters played by just two actors, hence the name. We really loved it and thought that it worked really well, but of course we didn't know what other people would think. With two people playing all these characters, it might come across as rushed, or confusing, we didn't know.

We premiered at the Bolton Octagon in the summer of 1990 and both John and I were petrified. In fact, we had been scared for weeks. In the middle of rehearsals we were sitting in the car park near the Octagon and I turned to John and said, 'Shall we ring Phil and tell him we'll just go back now?' We'd become a bit institutionalised if I'm honest. The comfort and safety of *Brookside* seemed preferable over the unknown of going onstage every night.

On opening night John and I stood backstage waiting to go on. I had a little peek as the auditorium filled up. It was a sell-out. The great thing about the fact that we were actors on *Brookside* was that people who wouldn't normally go to the theatre came to see us. They wanted to see what Sheila and Billy could do.

My friend Phil Thompson, the Liverpool footballing legend, isn't a theatre man at all but he came along. He called me in the afternoon before the show.

'Hi, Sue.'

He sounded downbeat. I was sure he was calling to say that he wasn't going to be able to make the performance.

'Everything all right, Phil?' I asked.

'Yeah. Fine...' He paused. 'Listen, this is going to sound a bit daft...but what do I wear to the theatre?'

I cracked up laughing. 'Wear what you want.'

'I don't need a penguin suit then?' he said, relief evident in his voice.

'Well, you can wear one if you want, but it's not a prerequisite...'

It was great to see so many people in the audience;

John and I just hoped we'd be able to give them their money's worth. As soon as I was onstage the nerves fell away and I felt like I did all those years ago when I was in Miss Potter's play at school. I was absolutely in the moment playing my characters, this was where I was happiest.

The play was extremely well received. John and I were thrilled. It was such a relief to get the first night over with and to look forward to the run. We went on to win the *Manchester Evening News* Theatre Award for best new play. After that, we took it to Edinburgh for the festival. We were again petrified as Andy told us that all the critics were in the audience. John's wife Kath had had enough of our anxieties by this time and said, 'It's been a success, you've had rave reviews, what's up with the pair of you?'

Again we got a great response at the festival. We were really pleased with what we'd achieved and when we went back to *Brookside* things never really felt the same again.

I wanted security for Joel but I really wasn't happy. Even the drive to work was getting me down: the same road, the same streets. I knew in my heart that I needed to move on. But the thought of being a jobbing actress again scared me.

A year after we premiered at the Octagon, John and I were approached to revive *Two* but this time after an initial run in Bolton we would transfer to the Young Vic theatre in London. I knew John had decided to leave. As the character he played was Sheila's love interest I felt that I couldn't bear to see her lose another man but I also knew that Phil Redmond wouldn't let me take another chunk of time out from *Brookside* to do it so I decided it was time for me to leave too.

I went to see Phil and told him of my intentions. At first he tried to persuade me to stay and offered me more episodes. We were all paid the same Equity rate at *Brookside*, but I could earn more money by being in more episodes. It wasn't about the money – it never really has been for me. Phil soon realised that I was ready to go and gave me his blessing. John and I left at the same time and had a joint leaving party. *Brookside* had changed my life and I will always be grateful to Phil for giving me my big TV break.

*

During this new run of *Two* one of the saddest and hardest things I have ever had to deal with happened. I was very close to a couple named Veron and Mike. I met them when I first worked at the Bolton Octagon, and they had a child, Dominic, who was six. They soon had a daughter, Gemma, who was born six months before Joel. Gemma and Joel used to play together all the time, and had a very special bond.

The family had always seemed to be a very solid unit, but later Mike got a job at the Crucible Theatre and they moved to Sheffield, and things started to unravel. Dom did well in his GCSEs but never really settled in his new school. Mike was spending more and more time away from the family at work and Veron was becoming increasingly lonely.

When Dominic went into sixth form he became very unhappy. There were a horrible few days when Dominic went missing. He turned up again, but it transpired that he had been smoking marijuana and then had taken magic mushrooms, which precipitated a breakdown in his mental health, and he was later admitted to a mental hospital where he was diagnosed with schizophrenia.

Instead of bringing Mike and Veron together to deal with what was happening with Dom, it drove a wedge between them: Veron felt very much like she was having to cope with this on her own, and she began to question their relationship. She found it very difficult that she and Mike seemed to have grown apart but she struggled with it as she was a Catholic and had been with Mike since she was a teenager, there had never been anyone else for her.

After much thought, Veron told Mike that she couldn't be with him any more. He was terribly angry and after one particularly horrible and bitter argument Veron went to the psychiatric unit to see Dom. Dom told her that his dad had already been in to see him. He didn't say what Mike had said to him.

Veron was meant to be coming to stay with me the

following day, a Friday evening. At about seven that evening I received a phone call from her.

'Sue,' she said flatly, 'I think you'd better sit down. Dom's dead.'

I let out a horrified gasp. She told me that after she had left Dom he had borrowed a pound from one of the other patients and used it to catch the bus into town, leaving a note in his room. He had then gone to the top of a high-rise block of flats and thrown himself off. I closed my eyes, horrified by the violence of his death, horrified by what Veron must be going through.

Veron was staying at her sister Di's in Sheffield and first thing the following morning I left Joel with my mum and dad and drove over.

Wordlessly, Veron looked at me, and I at her, and I held her. I could not comprehend what she was going through. She was so utterly in shock that it didn't feel like she was actually in the room. I saw Veron walk off; it was all too much for her. She went into the bathroom and then moments later we could hear a banging. She was keening, hitting her head against the wall.

Gemma was eleven at the time and it was awful for her to witness what was happening to her family. She asked if she could come back and stay with me and of course I said yes, and she came back with me for the week before the funeral.

The funeral was dreadful. It was in a beautiful country church. I can remember sitting outside in the car with my ex-husband Dave and smoking like a chimney. I had given up smoking a few years previously but the horror of what was happening had seen me reach for the fag packet.

We finally went into the church and I sat beside Margot and Dave. John Tams sang a beautiful song and I read the passage 'Footsteps'. I don't know how I kept my voice from cracking. When someone dies and they have lived to a grand old age, those gathered for the funeral can look back and celebrate their life. When someone dies so young and in such horrific circumstances there is none of that release. As Veron stood behind the coffin she let out a wail that seemed to come from the bottom of her soul. There was to be no respite from the grief for Veron. She was utterly devastated and blamed herself.

After the funeral, Veron would have the occasional good moment but on the whole she was in a trance, desperate for the pain to go away. I would take her hand and just let her say what she needed to say. I wasn't sure there was anything that I could say that would make things better.

A few short weeks after Dom's death I was invited to a party and Veron said that she would like to go, just to get out and to try to establish some kind of normality in her life again. We hadn't been there long when Veron asked if we could leave. We went back to my house.

That evening was awful, she kept saying that she could

see Dom at the end of a tunnel calling for her. The following morning as she walked away from me to leave she cut such a sad figure. She was wearing a brown linen Wallis dress and she looked beautiful, she really was very beautiful. That was the last time I saw her.

Less than a month after Dom's death Gemma went to stay with her father for the weekend. That night Veron wrote a letter asking that her sister Di and I would look after Gemma. She then took an overdose. My friend Romy called me the following day to tell me Veron had died. I couldn't quite take in what I was being told, I was utterly devastated.

A month to the day after Dom's funeral we were all back in the same church for his mother's funeral. Veron was buried in the same grave as Dom.

It was such an awful time for everyone involved but for Gemma, this poor little girl who was only eleven years old, it was absolutely devastating. I missed Veron but I was so terribly angry with her for leaving Gemma. Gemma went to live with her dad but she would also come and stay with Di and me. She always wanted to talk about her mum, she used to say, 'Didn't she love me as much as Dominic?' Of course she had loved Gemma with all her heart but that wasn't how it looked to her young daughter. Her mother couldn't live without her son so she took her life. Suicide leaves this huge question that is never answered which is why it is so hard for the people left behind to get over it.

Gradually, as Gemma has got older and matured, I think that she has come to understand the guilt and shame that her mum carried on her shoulders and why it had become too hard for her to live with. Veron blamed herself for the breakdown of her marriage and for Dom's death and didn't have the heart to go on. I've come to terms with that now. And I think Gemma has too.

Gemma really is the most amazing young woman. Despite all she has been through – which also included losing her father at nineteen in a tragic accident – she is a level-headed girl and a real beauty. When she got married I was so proud of her and I dearly wished that Veron and Mike could have been there to see her and share in her special day. Gemma is pregnant with her first baby, and I wish with all my heart that Veron could have held on, that we could somehow have got her through that pain. I just wish that there could have been some way to alter the course of events, to have Veron here with me now to share the joy of life with her. But I can't, so I will just say that Veron is still sorely missed by everyone whose life she touched.

Chapter Fifteen

AFTER I LEFT *Brookside* I felt free to do things that I wouldn't have been allowed to do while I was working on a long-running series. As well as *Two*, one of the other projects I took part in was a Radio 4 play set in a women's prison using the stories and voices of real women prisoners. This wasn't the first time that I would work in a prison. At M6 we had performed a play about the Peterloo Massacre at Strangeways. Strangeways is a huge Victorian prison in the middle of Manchester. It sits looking out of the north of the city as if as a reminder to the people of what grim fate awaits them if they step out of line. We were taken inside and into the prison chapel where we were to perform.

The prisoners were brought in and we were let loose on them. I was playing a toothless hag, my hair was all over the place, my clothes in tatters and as I came onto the stage the room erupted in wolf-whistles. I couldn't imagine how long these men must have gone without seeing a woman if what I was dressed as passed for sexy.

We launched into our play. Five minutes in, a guard blithely breezed past with scant regard for our performance and plonked a number where the hymn numbers should have been. 'Nice one,' a prisoner said, jumping up like he had a full house in Bingo, and he hurried past like he couldn't wait to get out of the room. Two minutes later the door opened again and the guard again heavy-footed across the wooden floor and stuck another number up. Again another prisoner was on his feet, pleased as punch that his number had been put up.

I came offstage and whispered to one of the guards, 'What's going on? What's with the numbers?'

He looked at me, he was about as impressed by our Brechtian theatre as the prisoners seemed to be. 'When the number goes up it means they've got a phone call. They're just glad to be out, to be honest.' My face must have fallen because he added, 'No offence.'

I don't think my appearance at Strangeways was my finest hour.

The time I would spend with the women in Styal Prison, recording the radio play, was a far more sobering experience. I was working with a group of actors including John McArdle again, and the director Kate Rowland.

We were taken through to the secure section where the women we would be interviewing were housed. They were Section 45 prisoners, sex offenders. These women were seen as pariahs by the other prisoners, their crimes such that they couldn't be kept near the others for fear of attack. While she was researching this play, Kate had spent a lot of time with these women. The script centred round a fictitious woman who was serving a life sentence but the women that Kate had interviewed were to play the extras.

As we walked towards the section the other prisoners began to shout to us, 'What you doing with them nonces? You should come and talk to us.'

We definitely felt some trepidation about the project we were embarking upon. We were introduced to the women that we would be working with during the next five days. In their cells were pictures of their children, some that they had been party to the abuse of or even killed. It was hard, but we had to try to disassociate ourselves from what had brought these women to this place and try to get the best out of them to make the play work.

The aim was that they would tell us their stories and then we would build it into the play. We wanted to know what being a female 'lifer' in prison was like. What we hadn't thought about was the amount of denial that these woman had about their crimes. They would begin to tell their stories and then tail off. A lot of them blamed their partners for the abuse they had been accused of but couldn't accept their part in it. Ironically, as the week went on the women began to trust us and open up to us, which was good for the project, but didn't sit easy with me at all, I didn't want to know the extent of why they were there – I didn't want to judge but I still had an opinion on what I heard.

Anyone who says that prison is an easy option can never have been inside one. The loss of liberty is always there. The clank of keys against locks a constant reminder of the fact that someone else is in charge of where you go and what you do. The cells are small and bare. The women had personalised them with pictures from home, but it seemed to me that this only served as a constant reminder of the crimes they had committed.

My lasting memory of working on that project was leaving those women after five days. We looked back and could just see these hands waving out of the cell doors. I found it terribly sad. I still think about them, and the fact that they were in there for life. I think about all I have experienced and seen since then, and that two decades later some of those women will still be there, in that same little space, contemplating what they did that brought them there.

We all went back to the BBC in Manchester and slumped into our chairs in the studio, not saying a word to one another. It was as if where we had been and what we had heard had just hit us. Kate opened a bottle of wine and gave us all a glass each and we drank it without speaking.

*

Later, I was sent a script for a three-part TV drama called *Goodbye Cruel World* written by Tony Marchant. I thought it was fantastic. I went to an interview with the producer David Snowdin and the director Adrian Shergold and read for the part, and when I arrived home my agent had already called to say that I had been offered the role – I was thrilled.

It was about a woman suffering from motor neurone disease, although we never said directly that that was what it was. We termed it 'Wey's Disease' – some symptoms we used might not have been experienced by someone with motor neurone disease and we didn't want to portray anything that wasn't factually correct. Alun Armstrong was to play my husband with Jonny Lee Miller as my son.

Motor neurone disease is degenerative, aggressive and fatal, attacking the neurones that control the motor function of the body. Alun and I met some amazing people with the disease during our research. One woman lived in a council house outside Oxford. She was very kind and hospitable to us and I thought it was extremely brave of her to let us in to see how she coped. She showed Alun how to pick her up and how to put her into the bed as I watched her intently, absorbing it all.

We went on to meet someone who told us how people dealt with MND psychologically. It is such an aggressive disease that the trauma of having to accept what is happening to you is often as bad as the physical symptoms. And we met the people whose lives had been turned on their head when their loved ones were diagnosed.

Alun is a brilliant actor and before *Goodbye Cruel World* had played Thénardier the Innkeeper in *Les*

Misérables. When we arrived at the hotel where we would be staying while we worked on the series, the door flew open and there stood the lady owner of the hotel resplendent in a *Les Mis* T-shirt. She looked at me for a split second and then realised that standing next to me was Alun Armstrong. 'Oh Alan!' she exclaimed in her strong Welsh accent. 'I loved you in *Les Misérables*.' She pointed at her T-shirt by way of demonstration.

She ushered us in and from then on she couldn't do enough for us. If one of us needed anything doing we would pretend it was for Alun and she would happily go off to fulfil our request, beaming from ear to ear in her freshly laundered *Les Mis* T-shirt. She really was the most lovely welcoming woman and even more so because we had the man who sang *Master of the House* with us.

Around this time my dad started to have problems with his health. He had contracted shingles and had been in such distress. I used go to see how he was and he would rub his head constantly, irritated by the pain. One evening as I was sitting in my room, learning my lines, I received a call from my mum. I was relieved as I'd been trying to get hold of her to see how Joel was. I'd called several times and it wasn't like my mother to not be in when she said she would. 'Hi, everything all right?' I asked, assuming that the answer would be, as it always was, 'yes'.

'Your dad's in hospital, Susan,' Mum said, sounding shocked. 'He's had a stroke.'

I couldn't believe it. Even with the shingles, I never thought of my dad as an invalid. It was too late to drive home so the following morning I was on set first thing. I told the director and the producer, who were very understanding, and I drove from Margate to Warrington. I had the soundtrack to *Les Misérables* in my car and I played it, crying all the way home. I needed my dad to be all right. I went back to Mum's and bought a potted plant as Dad liked plants and I didn't want to go to his bedside empty-handed, then I headed to the hospital.

I was shocked when I saw my dad. He was sitting in the bed, his face drooping to one side and his arm was paralysed. I couldn't believe it. I took his hand and sat down next to him. I'd recently been on holiday abroad and had bought my dad two hundred Benson & Hedges, but when I returned and he had shingles I didn't give them to him. When my mum went to the toilet, Dad leaned across and out of the corner of his mouth said, 'Have you brought those fags?'

Dad didn't have to stay long in hospital, which was a huge relief to me and I returned to Margate to finish filming. When I returned to Warrington, Dad was recovering well from the stroke. But the Benson & Hedges, it turned out, were playing heavily on his mind. One day I was at their house when I said that I was leaving to go into town. As I set off I decided to go straight home instead.

As I was in my lounge I looked out to see Dad's Allegro driving past the window and parking up. I waited in the hall as he let himself in, and seeing me he jumped a mile.

'What are you doing here?' he asked, clutching his chest. He was dressed in his pyjamas and his overcoat.

'I might ask you the same thing, sneaking around.'

Looking sheepish, he said, 'I've come for those fags.'

I shook my head. Those bloody fags. 'You're not having them,' I said. 'Not until your chest gets better.'

Dad went away fagless and fed up.

I did eventually relent. When his chest cleared up and he came looking for them again, I handed over the box and Dad opened a packet, took out a cigarette and, before lighting it, snapped off the filter tip. He was so used to strong untipped cigarettes that he thought that Benson & Hedges were too mild!

On one occasion when I was taking him home from a check-up Dad asked me to make a detour to the bank. My father had always handed over his wages every week to my mum and been given some spending money for the week. This was quite commonplace with people of their generation, the woman would take the money in order to run the house.

I wasn't sure what Dad could have wanted from the bank but when he came out he handed me three hundred pounds in cash. He had obviously been squirrelling this money away for years, unbeknownst to my mum, and now he wanted me to look after it. Dad and I shared a look of understanding: this had been my dad's bid for independence, something he had that was his own. We didn't speak about it again but I knew that he had withdrawn it because if anything happened to him, he didn't want this money to go unclaimed.

*

It seemed to take an age from the filming of *Goodbye Cruel World* to it being aired. During this downtime I threw myself into being with Joel. I would take him to school and pick him up, I'd spend my days cooking – looking through recipes to see what I could make and thinking about whom I could invite round to eat it. I spent time with my parents. But after a while the dread that I might never work again crept up on me. Usually I trusted that of course I would work again, that something would come up. But the part of me that knew that a few months out of work and I wouldn't be able to pay the mortgage was beginning to take over, and I became increasingly occupied by this concern. I decided that I would take whatever came up, that no part would be too small as it would mean that I could meet new people and hopefully gain work that way.

I had a part in *Inspector Morse*, which I was very pleased to get, although I did feel a bit cowed when John Thaw was taken in his big Jaguar car to set and I had to follow behind in a much less grand vehicle. I played Sean

Bean's older wife and had to sit at his bedside as he was stripped to the waist. I felt like ringing my agent and saying, 'Don't charge them for today, the pleasure was all mine!' Sean Bean is a lovely man and we chatted the day away about everything from the TUC to football – he is a passionate Sheffield Wednesday fan. I also worked on *A Touch of Frost*, which was in its first series at the time. I remember sitting in make-up alongside David Jason, wondering if I should say something. He felt like such a big star and me a jobbing actress. I decided to keep quiet and let the make-up girl get on with her job.

After this I filmed a play called *Bitter Harvest*, for the ITV series *Screenplay*, with Rudolph Walker and Josette Simon, which was shot in the Dominican Republic in 1992. It was a small crew and I was delighted to be working with some of the people from *Goodbye Cruel World*. We were staying in a five-star hotel but then we would go and film in places where people were suffering from the most abject poverty. It made you feel embarrassed that we were staying in such luxury while the locals had to live in squalor. Families were living next to a river that they used as their drinking well, laundry and toilet. Their houses were precariously perched on the banks and had to be moved when the river rose. I watched a little boy pulling around a plastic bottle with a piece of string tied to it as if it was the most treasured toy in the world. I really felt for these people.

To mark the five-hundredth anniversary of Christopher

Columbus discovering the Dominican Republic, the government had erected a huge cross on the coastline that could be seen from miles away at sea. It was illuminated, but the only problem was that every night when the cross was switched on, the lights went out across the island. Only buildings with their own generators were unaffected by this blackout.

We had a Winnebago with us, which I'm sure seemed rather grand to the locals, but when it refused to move we had to go cap in hand and ask if we could borrow some help to move it. One of the villagers kindly lent us his oxen, which dragged the Winnebago to the next location. It was such a fascinating place and the people were exceptionally friendly. We tried to get out as much as possible and I think that one of the advantages of filming somewhere like that is that you get to see the real unvarnished version of a place.

I returned home and after a few months *Goodbye Cruel World* finally aired. After the first episode finished the first person to call me was my dad. He told me how wonderful he thought it was and that he loved my performance and that he was very proud of me. I was so thrilled. To hear that from my dad meant more than any award in the world. He also said that my mum had enjoyed it, which was a relief.

The second episode, screened the following week, didn't fare quite so highly in my mother's estimation. In fact, it went down like a lead balloon. I knew when they didn't call that my mother probably wasn't happy. There was a scene in which I was in the bath naked and I thought that must be what had pushed her over the edge. I picked the phone up and called.

'Dad, it's me...' I said nervously.

There was a pause and then Dad said gravely, 'I think you'd better come and see your mother. It was the swearing, Sue, she really didn't like the swearing.'

I'd said 'fuck' twice, or rather my character had. A woman with motor neurone disease had said fuck twice as all control over her faculties left her – it seems reasonable enough in the circumstances, but try explaining that to my mother!

I went round to see Mum, she was sitting there, arms crossed, her face set as if she'd just sucked a lemon.

'Well,' she said, with utter disapproval, 'I don't know how you expect me to go into the post office again after that!'

When my mother was alive, the family would watch anything that I was in on two levels: for the programme itself and for my mother's reaction. They all said that they watched *Goodbye Cruel World* with hoots of laughter, knowing that my mother would be horrified with me, boobs akimbo, swearing like a navvy.

Later that year I was nominated for the *Radio Times* Performance of the Year Award for the role. The ceremony took place at lunchtime and I was absolutely thrilled to win it. I called Dad and told him. He went quiet for a moment and then said how pleased he was for me. He was a man of few words, my dad, but I could hear it in his voice, he was very proud. Then he said, 'I'll tell your mother, she'll be pleased.' At least an award might see my mum venturing to the post office again.

I used to give any awards I received to my mother. She liked to have them around her house. Although she could never articulate the fact that she was proud of me, and would often be close to despair when people asked her if she was, little things like this suggested that she might have been.

*

I had been worried about work for some time, as nothing regular had come up, so I was immensely pleased when I was offered a part in a series called *Medics*. I played the administrator Ruth Parry, opposite 'general surgeon' Tom Baker, and it was to film in Manchester, which was great for me as it was near to home and my family.

Soon after we began work on *Medics* my dad started to suffer from chest pains. Dad was the opposite of my mother. She had spent much of her life suffering from respiratory problems and being happy to be indulged because of her asthma. Dad hated being ill and really resisted it; like me he would go to bed and hide until he was better. So to hear him complain that he had chest pains I knew that he must be ill.

The fact that Dad was poorly didn't stop my mum insisting on him doing his quota of 'jobs' though. I went round to the house one day, to find my ailing father on his hands and knees scrubbing the kitchen floor.

'Dad!' I exclaimed, horrified. 'What are you doing?'

He knelt up with the scrubbing brush in his hand and wiped his brow. 'You know what your mother's like if the kitchen floor isn't done.'

I was livid: to hell with the kitchen floor – Dad wasn't well!

The doctor referred Dad to the hospital and he was X-rayed to see if they could pick anything up. They found a shadow on his lung. I could tell that Dad was very frightened. They told my dad he had cancer, and that it had spread to his bones. The consultant explained that he would undergo radiotherapy, with the reassuring words that 'In six weeks, Fred, you'll see a difference.'

I'm not sure if this doctor knew that dad was dying and just wanted to give him some hope or genuinely thought that the treatment would work. Dad was given morphine to take at home to ease the pain and I would ferry him to the hospital to receive his radiotherapy.

Towards the end of his six weeks of treatment my dad's condition suddenly deteriorated. We arrived at the hospital but the doctor on admissions insisted that Dad have an X-ray. My father was crying out in pain but this man was obviously keen to tick his procedural boxes. I tried to reason with him, but he wasn't listening. By chance, the doctor who had diagnosed my father with cancer was passing by. I threw myself on his mercy, pleading with him to give my dad some pain relief. He quickly administered some morphine. I was so thankful to him for easing the pain of a dying man. My father was admitted straight away but I was so angry with the other doctor, in fact, I still feel that way now – how dare he ignore my dad's pain in that way?

I was at my dad's bedside for the last three days of his life. Just before I made that final trip to the hospital I had woken up that morning and put on Veron's brown Wallis dress, the last thing I saw her wear. Her sister Di had given it to me after Veron died and this was a thing that I had treasured but never yet worn. I've no idea why I was drawn to it that day, I think it was a way of me feeling protected by my friend, of wrapping her around me.

It was close to Christmas and outside there was a holiday feeling in the air, carol singers came on the ward and I popped out to hear them sing. I cried as I listened to the singers, knowing that Christmas was so near but feeling sure that my dad would not be with us by then. Gradually, Dad lost consciousness.

I was sitting at his side looking at him, in profile he had a large nose and as he had lost so much weight his features were sunken. I squeezed his hand. 'Bloody hell, Dad, you look just like Geronimo.' I was thinking of the pictures of the Native American I had seen with his prominent nose, small eyes and shrivelled skin.

Dad laughed faintly and said slowly, 'I feel like bloody Geronimo.'

In these last few days he rarely spoke as he was so heavily sedated. At one point he suddenly sat bolt upright in bed, his big blue eyes open wide, and said, 'Mam!' He then slumped back into the bed and into sleep. His breathing became extremely laboured and I began to worry that he had stopped breathing altogether. I hovered over him, and then his chest rose; I could relax a little. I began to count the seconds between each breath and got to eighty-nine at one stage. I was very close to running and grabbing a nurse when his chest rose again.

I had such an intense love for my dad and really needed to be by his side. I cried so much in those final days, but as with my mother I was privileged to have this time with my dad. I told him that I loved him and chatted to him. During this time his next-door neighbour Peter came in every day and chatted to him about his garden. Dad had always loved his plants and Peter was a professional gardener so they would swap tips. When I was younger we had the most wonderful garden with herbaceous borders running down the side and red-hot pokers spiking out of the flowerbeds. Dad had a greenhouse where he would grow tomatoes and cucumbers and chat to the resident frog who, like my dad, was named Fred. He then built a pond and we had goldfish swimming around in it. It was a little oasis for my dad. Even now that he was older he loved his garden and it was still a little place for him to escape to.

Joel came in to see him but he found it difficult to see his grandad so ill; he had always been more like his father than his grandfather. My mum came in every day but it was so overwhelming for her, I really felt so sorry for her.

On the third day of sitting by my dad's side in Veron's dress, my mum and Aunty Millie came in to see him. Joel had been dropped off at the hospital by a friend and I decided that I would take Joel home and have a shower. I have no idea why I chose that moment but when I arrived home I received a call saying that Dad had gone into a steep decline. I jumped back in the car with Joel and drove like a bat out of hell. The traffic was ridiculous and I weaved around cars, shouting in frustration at the traffic, but I was more frustrated at myself for leaving the hospital when I did.

When I arrived, I ran to the nurses' station. I could tell by the look on the sister's face that it was bad news. 'I'm sorry, Sue,' she said. 'Your dad has passed away.'

I was distraught; I should have been there.

'We see this a lot, you know,' the nurse explained gently. 'He might not have wanted you to see him die.'

I thought about this and realised that there might be some truth in what she was saying, but I don't think it was me he would have been worried about; it was Joel. Joel was so special to my dad that I think he would have done whatever he could to make sure that Joel wasn't upset in any way.

I went into the room and Dad was lying in the bed, my mum and Aunty Millie at his side.

'Touch him, Sue, he's still warm,' Aunty Millie said.

I think she just needed something to say and this was what she arrived at! I kissed him, and then stood back and looked at him. It wasn't my dad, it was his body lying there, but it wasn't him. It was then that I realised that our bodies are really just what carries us, our essence, around – a shell. My dad had gone, but where? Where had all that knowledge, that humour, that gentleness gone? Mum and Aunty Millie went to the visitors' day room for a cup of tea and I stayed with Dad, but after a while I knew I had to leave. I felt awful saying goodbye for the last time.

The following day I went to pick up the death certificate from the hospital and was given two carrier bags that held Dad's stuff. I took the bags home and put them in his shed and didn't look at them for eighteen months. When I finally did, I salvaged his watch and his slippers, which I still occasionally wear now. I went with my uncle Gordon to the registry office to register Dad's death. We were sitting there waiting our turn, Christmas decorations hanging on the wall. I felt shocking, as if I was dreaming, as if everyone else was going about their lives around me and I was just standing still.

As we sat there in silence, a woman leaned over and said, 'Are you who I think you are?' She paused as I looked blankly at her. 'It's Sheila Grant, isn't it?'

This really wasn't a good time to be recognised. I nodded that I was as Gordon stared at her, trying to get her to twig that I was upset and didn't really want to have a chat about my days on *Brookside*.

Dad died on 21 December 1993. I was convinced that we would have to wait until after Christmas for the funeral, but we were told that there was a space on Christmas Eve. I discussed it with my mum and we decided to take it.

I began ringing around to see if there was anywhere we might have the wake but of course everywhere was filled with Christmas bookings. In the end, my friends Dean and Janice organised a buffet for us and set it all up while we were at the church. I was so thankful to them for doing that. At the church we sang 'In the Bleak Midwinter' and my father's favourite poem, 'A Shropshire Lad', was read. At the crematorium they played 'To Be A Pilgrim', which made me smile sadly as I thought about my dad – one of the silly little things he would do was to change the words around so that he sang, 'To Be a Grim Pill'. Another thing that my dad used to say which always sticks with me is 'From the sublime to the cor blimey' instead of 'From the sublime to the ridiculous'. His funny little sayings used to make me laugh and it made me upset that I'd never hear him say those words again.

At the end of the service they played 'You'll Never Walk Alone'. I was distraught hearing this Liverpool anthem and thinking about how much my dad meant to me. I knew I should be getting out of my seat to speak to people and thank them for coming but I just sat there sobbing.

Afterwards everyone came back to my mum's; Dean and Janice had done us proud. They had put on a wonderful spread and I felt very much supported by my great friends and family. After a while I noticed that Joel wasn't around and I went to find out where he'd gone. He was sitting on the edge of my dad's bed.

'Joel, are you all right?' I asked. I knew how hard this was for him.

He nodded his head, then after a bit of thought said, 'Mum, can we start Christmas now?'

Poor Joel, all this sadness and focus on my dad's funeral had totally taken away from any Christmas preparations. My dad would have agreed with Joel; he loved Christmas and loved to see Joel's face when he opened his presents. I gave my son a hug and a kiss and said, 'Course we can.'

Mum, Joel and I had a quiet, sad Christmas together. We didn't know what to do with ourselves – Dad's death was so recent and we missed him desperately. But my mother and I gave Joel his presents and tried to make sure that he didn't miss out on the day.

My friend Susie Mathis saw how desperate we all were and invited us around for Boxing Day. That year she really made Boxing Day our Christmas. Susie is a very dear friend and has always been a brilliant character. At the time she hosted the morning breakfast show at Piccadilly radio in Manchester and was great at throwing a party – she still is. This was the first time that my mother had met Susie and Susie's language can be a little, shall we say…colourful. Susie sat there effing and jeffing and my mum sat at the other end of the table open-mouthed: I watched with a mixture of horror and enjoyment. I have always been so careful not to upset my mum by swearing or saying anything that might offend her, and to have someone who was so confident and comfortable in her use of profanity was something of a joy to behold!

The party was great and Joel got the Christmas he needed and deserved. Bryan Robson came with his wife Denise and Joel beat him at chess. Bryan approaches everything he does with the attitude that he is going to win, be that football or tiddly winks, so to be beaten by a boy at chess came as something of a shock! We of course all thought it was fabulous and cheered Joel in his victory. Steve and Jan Bruce were there and other friends of Susie's popped in from the village. My mum didn't really drink but Susie was topping her lemonade up with wine. We were all still very much in shock from Dad's death but this gathering helped us come back into the world a little after the awful few weeks we'd had.

I went back to work on *Medics* the following week and Tom Baker said, 'Come here, my little orphan,' and gave me a big hug. I felt very lucky to be working on that job in Manchester. All of the cast and crew were lovely and very understanding and I was so grateful to be near to my mum.

*

I tried to get on with life, my mum needed me and Joel needed me, I didn't feel I had time to grieve for my dad. I knew that I missed him dreadfully but I thought my role was to just get on with it, so that's what I tried to do. I didn't want to show anyone how upset I was, least of all myself. I was so thankful that I had had a very special relationship with my dad. I didn't want to spoil this by being upset about it. I now know that grief will always find a way out but I am still very grateful for the time I had with such a special man.

Chapter Sixteen

FOR THE NEXT year and a half after my dad's death I tried to get on with life as best I could. I was looking after my mother, looking after Joel, and working on *Medics*. I didn't feel like I had time for myself but that was fine as I think I was aware that as soon as I stopped, the fragile edifice I had constructed around me in a bid to ignore the grief I felt at my father's death would come crashing down around me.

It was around this time that I took a step away from the Labour Party – or perhaps it is more correct to say that the Labour Party took a step away from me! I had always been happy to go along to Labour events to speak or just show my support and as such had been approached by the group Arts for Labour, who involved people in the arts and media with the party.

After the shock death of John Smith, the party needed a new leader. Seventeen years on, it is well known that some sort of deal was struck between Tony Blair and Gordon Brown and that the job of Leader of the Opposition went to the slicker, New Labour Blair in July

1994. At the time this wasn't common knowledge, but I did think that within the walls of the party it was an acknowledged fact.

Shortly after Blair became leader I was asked by Arts for Labour if I would go along to one of their events. My role would be to make a little speech and then invite Gordon Brown on to the stage to address the party faithful.

I arrived at the venue and it was a lovely summer's evening. There was an air of genuine optimism in the room and I have to say I felt buoyed by it. Labour seemed to be getting itself into shape for the next general election after the severe bruising it had taken in 1992. Everyone was extremely lovely to me when I arrived, chatting away, saying how pleased they were that I could make it. I felt very much welcomed. Peter Mandelson was there, keeping a beady eye on everything, but I wasn't introduced to him.

I went up onstage, said my little bit, and then I said, 'I'd like to welcome Gordon Brown onto the stage and I'm sure that everyone will join with me in thanking him for stepping aside in the bid for the leadership in order to not cause a rift in the party.'

There was stunned silence in the room. I had obviously said something that no one was supposed to acknowledge. I had mentioned the war! I felt tumbleweed rolling past my feet. Gordon Brown came on the stage with a tight smile and I was ushered off. After he spoke, everyone in the room literally turned their backs on me. It was the most extraordinary thing. An aide approached me and said simply, 'Your car is ready.' They couldn't have got rid of me quicker if they'd fired me out of a cannon!

The following day the woman from Arts for Labour who had asked me to go along to the event called. 'What on earth did you say to Peter Mandelson?' she asked.

'I didn't say anything,' I assured her. 'I didn't even speak to him!'

'Well, he completely lost it,' she informed me. 'He was shouting afterwards, "How was that allowed to happen? No one vetted her speech!"'

I was horrified. I suppose I was given a glimpse of what was to come. Up until then I had always seen the Labour Party as somewhere you were encouraged to speak freely, but this was the beginning of the era of 'spin'. After that, I was occasionally asked to go along to Arts for Labour events but I didn't feel that I could. The incident had soured things for me. I hadn't meant any disrespect to Gordon Brown and have always thought that he was a lovely man; I was just stating what I saw as the truth.

Having never met Mandelson before, our paths didn't cross again throughout Labour's time in power. The other year, however, I was lucky enough to get tickets to the filming of *Strictly Come Dancing*. Who should be sitting behind me but Peter Mandelson! I'm not sure if he knew who I was but I gave him a vinegar look my mother would have been proud of. I have to say he seemed to be

enjoying the dancing far more than he enjoyed my introduction to Gordon Brown!

*

At this time I was continuing to feel the loss of my father
terribly but still not acknowledging it to myself. Joel was
a teenager and the last thing I thought he needed was his
mum falling to pieces. Also, my mother was struggling
and leaning heavily on me. She missed my dad dreadfully.

My dad had always done everything for her. He did all
of the jobs around the house, cleaned the car, scrubbed
the floor and tended the garden. He also cooked and used
to make a great Sunday roast. Dad had been in the
catering corps for some of his time in the army and had
learned to cook there. It might have been unusual for a
man of his generation, but Dad enjoyed it and was good
at it, so it was just normal in our house. After he died, my
mum tried to rewrite history and claim that it was she
who'd done it all.

'He never cleaned that car, it was always me,' she
would inform me.

And I can't remember ever seeing my mother look for
her own handbag when my dad was around. 'Fred,
where's my handbag?' she would demand.

Dad would go in search of it for her.

'Here you go, Margaret,' he would say without a note
of complaint in his voice, he was so used to his role as
Chief Handbag Fetcher, poor man.

In *Two* with John
McArdle, in 1989

Goodbye Cruel World
with Alun Armstrong,
and a very young
Jonny Lee Miller

A big hug from Tom Baker
(while filming *Medics*)

Mary Healey and me looking marvellous
in make-up for *Brassed Off*

The amazing cast of *Brassed Off*

It was an honour to play
Pat Phoenix

The wonderful *Royle Family*

With Ricky at a *Royle Family* charity event for the Kirsty Appeal

Dean Sullivan could always charm my mother

'How old do you think I am, Millie?' Albert Finney with my aunty

Me as nurse Sal with the rest of the *Jam and Jerusalem* cast – I don't think we ever stopped laughing when we were filming this

In make-up, Trevor
Eve drops by

This was the final scene ever of *Waking the Dead*, taken under Waterloo Bridge

Dad and Mum together in their early seventies

With my mum on her ninetieth birthday

The photo we faked for my mother of Joel's graduation day

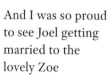

Laughter is the best policy, with Susie

Receiving my OBE – my mother
would have been so proud

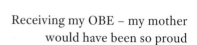

And I was so proud
to see Joel getting
married to the
lovely Zoe

There was no one in my life that I could take any of my own thoughts and feelings to about my dad so I just bottled them up. There were times when I did try to speak to my mum about it. 'Mum…' I'd begin tentatively. She would eye me as if to say, *what's coming here?* 'I've been thinking about Dad…'

Mum would immediately be up out of the chair, busying herself so that we didn't have to have a conversation that she didn't want.

'Mum, are you listening?' I would say, trying to persevere.

'Are we having a cup of tea?' she'd ask, making it clear that she wasn't prepared to have a conversation about my father. I found this very sad but I knew my mother so well: she wasn't the sort of person who was going to have a heart to heart just because I wanted one.

I began to feel extremely low again and after eighteen months I hit a wall and slumped back into utter despondency: my depression was back. No one who was working with me at that time would have known that I was depressed as I was now adept at putting on a mask and pretending that everything was normal. My self-esteem was very low at this time and I began to feel quite worthless. I would look at people and wish that I could be as carefree as them. At the same time I would berate myself, 'What have you got to worry about? You've got a good job, a good home, a lovely son. You haven't anything to be depressed about.' Classic depressive behaviour really, but when you're in the thick of it it's hard to see.

When *Medics* came to an end it compounded these feelings of worthlessness. Someone else was in control of my life, not me. I didn't feel I had the power to affect my destiny as an actress; I was always at the mercy of the people who made the decisions. I was again waiting at home to see if anyone would call to give me a role. I had moved into a different age group, as far as parts were concerned. I was in my early fifties and I do think that at this age a lot of women disappear. We have seen it recently with the case of BBC presenters being supplanted by younger models. As an actress I was very aware of this. I went to look at small flats near Joel's school, sure that I wouldn't be able to continue to pay the mortgage on my house.

Mum had begun to bounce back at about the same time that my dad's death was finally hitting me. She was getting out more with her brothers and sisters, and their bond, which had always been tight, became stronger. They would go on days out together and fill their time well with activities.

I had begun to avoid calls and to stay in bed when Joel was at school. I didn't feel like I wanted to be part of the world and eventually I had to admit I needed help. I hauled myself out of the house and went to the doctor's and told him of the bleak time I was having and I was put on antidepressants again. I just wanted it all to go away but I knew that when I felt like this I had to face it head on. I finally came out of the blackness and felt a little more like myself again but of course something was missing and that something was my dad.

I needed something to take me out of myself and by serendipity I was asked by Comic Relief to go to South Africa to film and see first-hand some of the work they were doing there. From its inception in 1989 I had witnessed the great work that Comic Relief was doing. I think there is a common misconception that Comic Relief's work is solely focused on Africa, but in fact much of the money supports charities in the UK, and I had visited refuges in the UK where women who suffered from domestic violence were given a safe place to stay, counselling and support. On this occasion, though, I would be seeing how the money was spent in Africa.

Joel was sixteen so I took him with me. For both of us it was to be the most amazing, eye-opening trip.

*

We were taken to the constitutional courts in Johannesburg where we met Albie Sachs. Before the abolition of apartheid I had been horrified by what was happening in South Africa. Albie Sachs was a prominent freedom fighter during the era of apartheid. He had been imprisoned alongside Nelson Mandela on Robben Island. To meet this man meant a great deal to me, he had been through so much – losing an arm and the sight in one eye after a bomb that had been left in his car by government security agents exploded. He was now a judge and was overseeing the new courts and the reinstatement of land to people who had been dispossessed.

He was only meant to be with us for half an hour but I think he realised how interested and passionate we were about what he was doing that he stayed with us all morning. I tried to impress upon Joel what an honour this was, and who this man was. In the eighties I had been a member of the ANC, but I had always felt slightly ineffectual. I wasn't really sure what me trying to stop people from buying grapefruit really achieved, but we just wanted to bring awareness to the cause. As far as I was concerned, our government turned a blind eye to apartheid for many years. Now I could see that even if all we did was raise awareness then it helped in a small way to throw light on what had been happening in this country.

After this we were taken to the townships and saw first-hand the poverty in which these people were living. After the abolition of apartheid large towns had been built to house black communities but they were so far out of the city that they were effectively another form of segregation. Soon people began to move back nearer the city and the townships expanded again.

We went to an old concrete factory that was now being used as accommodation. As we climbed out of the car a group of locals were there to greet us, singing a beautiful, harmonious a cappella song. Inside the factory were small, uninhabitable rooms with entire families living in them. The only sanitation was an open sewer that ran past the factory. The residents took us to see a toilet that had been built using Comic Relief money. We were led through into a room and shown a pristine toilet. It looked like it had never been used and polished for days.

We were stopped by some of the women as we left. One asked, 'Please can you send more? We need help, you have seen how we are living.'

She was right and I felt terrible that I personally couldn't do more.

She explained that the building of the toilet meant so much to them but they needed far more help than just one toilet – all we had to do was look around.

Next we went to an orphanage where the children there were orphans of parents who had contracted AIDS. The children were talking about their lives and there was an overwhelming sadness that came across. Kevin Cahill, the Comic Relief chief executive, was with us. The children had been telling their stories, there was so much grief and sadness in the room that he wanted to see if there was anything to distract them from their sorrow. He asked the children, 'What makes you happy?'

They looked back at him blankly with these huge, sorrowful eyes. They had no answer for him. It was heartbreaking.

Steve Redgrave, the Olympic rower, was also with us. We had noticed that the children didn't have footballs and would chase around carrier bags that had been tightly bound with twine. We had brought footballs to give out to the children on our travels and had one left. Steve went around the back of the orphanage and threw it into the field where the children were playing. There was almost a riot! These children were so pleased with such a small thing.

It really made me feel grateful for everything I had and to appreciate how lucky we are to be born in this country. After Steve gave them the gift of a ball they asked us to sing for them. Everywhere we had gone we had been greeted by beautiful harmonious song. We looked at one another, not knowing what to sing, and someone suggested 'Away in a Manger'. So in the blistering African heat we began to sing a Christmas carol in our flat, British voices. The kids and their carers all looked at one another like they wished they hadn't bothered asking!

Next we were taken to an AIDS clinic, which was attached to the orphanage. It had been built using Comic Relief money. I was asked to sit in with one of the nurses. It seemed to me that AIDS was the biggest problem faced by ordinary women in South Africa. There was such ignorance around the disease. People would rather believe that they had TB, as the symptoms were similar, rather than face an HIV test and live with the shame of this. Antiretroviral drugs were available but in order to be treated with them you had to be diagnosed as HIV positive. The saddest and most frustrating thing for me was that the women who had HIV had, on the whole, contracted the disease through their partner, who had concealed their infidelities from them. Culturally, the use of condoms was shunned. It was a desperate situation.

I was sitting in the room when a woman came in for the results of her blood test. She was a young mother and had one son with her, she had left her other children at home. I asked about her personal circumstances. She explained that her husband had left her and she was now bringing her children up with the help of her mother. This was a recurring tale: I met many women who had been left by their men to bring up their children alone.

'You're HIV positive,' the nurse said, leaning in to take the woman's hand. She sat emotionless, staring at the wall. I felt like an unwanted presence, a shadow on the wall. I was totally uncomfortable being there as this woman received this devastating news.

'My son?' she asked.

The nurse looked at her compassionately before giving her the devastating news: 'He's positive too.'

She told the woman to go home and get her other children and bring them back for tests. I went away extremely saddened. But I was more convinced than ever that the work of Comic Relief was essential. If it could raise awareness about AIDS and prevent one other woman from going through what I had just witnessed, then its work was necessary.

One of the things that struck me most about the villages we visited was that there almost seemed to be a missing generation: grandparents were bringing up young children because their parents had died of AIDS. It was extraordinary and very sad.

Joel wasn't the most expressive of teenagers but he was deeply touched by what he witnessed and I sensed that it was as much a privilege for him to go to South Africa as it was for me. He had taken his camera and took some amazing pictures of our travels.

*

Around this time I was approached about a role in a film about a group of miners who played in the colliery brass band as the pit is being forced into closure. After my involvement with the miners' strike, the subject was very close to my heart. The film was *Brassed Off*.

Brassed Off was the first feature film I had been involved in. I went to meet the director Mark Herman and told him that I loved the script. I was offered the part later that day and I couldn't have been happier.

Pete Postlethwaite had already signed up to be in the film and I was tremendously excited about having the opportunity to meet him and work with him. Pete and I had been born a few streets apart in Warrington but until now our paths had never crossed. This was amazing really, seeing as our families knew one another – Pete's niece lived next door to my cousin – and they would meet at events held at St Oswald's club in Padgate Lane where my aunty Jean used to go to play bingo. Aunty Jean would let them know what I was up to and they in turn would say what Pete was working on. The fact that we were both actors didn't concern them a jot. They'd have had the same conversation if we both worked on the bins.

On the first day of filming I walked into the foyer of the hotel in Doncaster where we would be staying for the next few weeks, ready to introduce myself to everyone. Pete Poss, Phil Jackson, Jim Carter and Stephen Tompkinson were all sitting there.

'Hi!' I said cheerfully.

'Hi, Sue,' they all said in unison.

I sat down.

'We're just talking about the rugby,' Pete said.

There had been a big England game that day. I'd just seen the result. Great, I thought, smashing icebreaker. 'We did well to win, didn't we?'

There was a collective groan.

'Bloody hell, Sue!' Pete said, laughing.

I looked around, perplexed. What had I done?

They had all been holding off finding out the score and had wanted to watch the match on the TV later.

'Oh no! I'm so sorry,' I said. 'Shall I just go back out, come back in and start again?'

So much for my icebreaker! I thought I might have ostracised myself with my big gob. It wasn't the case, we soon all became firm friends and had a great time making the film.

We became regulars at the local pub and formed our own quiz team. Ewan McGregor had been in the huge hit *Trainspotting* the year before and had a gaggle of teenage admirers wherever we went. The fire alarm for the hotel would often be set off in the middle of the night and young girls would be hanging around, waiting to get a glimpse of Ewan, freezing in his pyjamas on the street.

We filmed in Grimethorpe near Doncaster, although in the film the place was called Grimley. On the first day of filming we went into a room where the real colliery band were all waiting for us. We all gathered around and then they played for us: the music was magical. There is something especially rousing and proud about a brass band. Especially when it is a community group.

When they had finished, the band leader turned to us and said, 'Right, your turn.'

We all looked at one another and I took a step to one side, I wasn't in the band in the film so thankfully I was off the hook. The men who were in the band, and Tara Fitzgerald who was to play the only woman member, sat down and tried to play. It wasn't the most harmonious brass band you've ever heard but for a first attempt it wasn't bad!

As filming progressed everyone in the band got better and better at playing their instruments, which I thought was a testimony to the importance of the band in the film and what it meant to the actors to do justice to their parts. Pete played Danny, the conductor. Having never conducted so much as a bus, Pete took up the baton like he'd been doing it all his life. In the film he totally embodies the part, the music takes him over, the pit and the band mean so much to him.

We spent a lot of time in Grimethorpe and met lots of families who had lived through the strikes and the pit closures. There was still deep resentment for Margaret Thatcher. It was felt that the government had closed the pits but hadn't offered any alternative. I was seeing first-hand the effects of the Tory policy of mine closures that had been so hard fought over in the eighties. These towns that had only one major industry to support them now had nothing. With their industry crushed, people had no alternative but to sign on the dole. In Grimethorpe, a little over ten years on from the first of the eighties miners' strikes, the fallout was clear. Unemployment was high; there were drug and drink problems among the youth; buildings that had once thrived with life were derelict, their windows smashed, the land they stood on overgrown with weeds. There was a shiny new uninhabited community centre but it felt like too little too late.

At the end of *Brassed Off*, the Colliery Band go to the Royal Albert Hall to be in the Band of the Year competition. When it is announced that they have won, Pete's character, Danny, stands up and makes an impassioned speech declining the award. This has gone on to be one of the most memorable speeches in British cinema. Before it was filmed Mark the director gathered us all round and said that he wasn't going to do a run-through. Pete was going to do one speech and that was the one he would use in the film.

Pete took to the rostrum, looked out at the audience and began speaking. A silence fell across the room, everyone felt the words. It encapsulated everything I felt about the miners' strike.

In the last ten years this bloody government has systematically destroyed an entire industry. *Our industry*. And not just our industry: our communities, our homes, our lives. All in the name of progress and for a few lousy bob.

Danny's anger, *Pete*'s anger, was palpable. The Grimethorpe band were in the background as extras, I saw their heads bow, it was such a powerful, heart-breaking speech, and I can't think of another actor who could have made it with such force and passion.

We finished filming and all said our goodbyes, off to work on other projects. I never know if something I have been in will be a success, I have no barometer for that sort of thing. I just knew that I'd really enjoyed myself and hoped that it would be well received when it eventually saw the light of day.

Brassed Off was released in cinemas and was a huge hit. It is great to have been part of such a fabulous project with such a wonderful cast and crew and I feel it was not only an uplifting film but also an accurate depiction of the effects of Mrs Thatcher's brutal policy and the miners' strike.

When Pete died earlier this year I was terribly sad. He was such a lovely man and it was a great loss to not only his friends and family but to the world of theatre and film when he passed away. I went to his memorial service at St Leonard's church in Shoreditch. The Grimethorpe Colliery band were there, and when they played 'Danny Boy' it was especially poignant. Pete had never stopped supporting them and always went to see them when he was up north. At the end of the service Pete's voice boomed out over the speakers, he was reading the poem 'A Shropshire Lad', the poem that had been my dad's favourite and was read at his funeral. It made me very sad to think again of my father and those verses that he loved so much. And to think of Pete. The service was a beautiful and moving tribute to a truly great man.

Chapter Seventeen

WHEN JOEL WAS eighteen he got a place at college studying graphic design. Having always been sure that when he left home I would not behave the way my own mother had, and declare that my life was over, I was shocked to find how upset I was.

I drove him to Wrexham, which would be his new home, and helped him unpack his belongings. As we sorted out his room, some of the other lads who Joel would share the house with, and who would become his great friends, came in and introduced themselves. I was happy that he was about to embark on a new adventure but I have to admit I was bereft. I drove home in tears.

Once home I took the dogs out for a walk but felt totally despondent. Without Joel to go home to I couldn't help thinking, 'What's the point?'

I thought things might improve the next day but I awoke still feeling desolate. I passed a young woman pushing a pram and I began to cry. I was a wreck. Susie called in and seeing my face all puffed up asked quite reasonably, 'What are you crying for?'

'It's Joel...' I said, descending into tears again before I could finish my sentence.

'What's happened?' Susie asked, looking alarmed.

'Nothing, it's just he's gone, hasn't he?' I sobbed.

Susie was trying to be as diplomatic as possible but I think she thought I'd gone mad. After a few moments of obviously thinking, how do I put this?, she said, 'He's back on Friday, isn't he?'

I nodded, still crying. Yes, he was back on Friday, in three days' time! I knew I was being ridiculous but I missed him. He might only be in Wrexham and only away during the week but he wasn't living with me now and even though he hadn't been a little boy for a long time he wasn't *my* little boy any more. It wasn't the first stage of letting go, I felt that I'd been building to this from the first time he hadn't wanted to hold my hand as a little boy but still, I felt it deeply.

I soon got used to the fact that Joel was at college and would look forward to the times he was home, hearing about his course and his new friends, but I threw myself into work again and was very glad that I had my career to take my mind off how much I missed my son.

Suddenly, I began to understand what my mother had gone through. When she was raising me, I was her life. Joel is the most important person to me in the world, but I had a career that I'd maintained throughout his child-hood, so when he left home I had something else to be getting on with. And there was also the fact that I didn't tell Joel how I was feeling, whereas my mother had no qualms about telling me!

It was around this time that I was asked by Ron Rose, a northern writer who had worked at the Bolton Octagon, if I would play Pat Phoenix in *The Things You Do For Love*. Having met – and been overawed by – the woman herself I readily agreed.

I had never taken on the role of someone real before, and I certainly wasn't an impersonator, so I sat down and watched hours of footage of her, trying to get her manner and her character right. I learned a lot about her that I hadn't known. She had had a tempestuous relationship with Tony Booth, Cherie Blair's father, an actor famous for his role as the 'Scouse Git' in *Till Death Us Do Part*.

Tony was involved in a terrible accident where he was horribly burned and scarred, and returned to Pat on his uppers. She took him in and looked after him. After this, she herself contracted lung cancer and we filmed at the hospital where she had been nursed.

She had been a lifelong heavy smoker and even in her hospital bed she had an ashtray. She would puff on her cigarettes and then drag on her ventilator.

I met one of the nurses who had looked after her in her final weeks. 'Why did you allow her to smoke when she was so ill?' I asked. I wasn't being facetious, I was genuinely interested.

'It was her only pleasure,' she admitted. 'We just

thought there was no point in denying her something she enjoyed so much in her final days.'

Pat married Tony Booth on her deathbed. She lasted another eight days and died in her sleep. She had been such a vibrant, strong woman and her love for this man had spanned her life. I thought it was a very moving story.

Early one Sunday morning I was getting ready to go to set when I heard the news reporter talking about a princess who had been seriously injured in a car crash. They were reporting from Paris and I assumed that it was a European princess they were talking about. When I got in the car to go to work the driver informed me that the princess they had been referring to was Diana. I was horrified and listened transfixed to the radio.

On set, one of the crew set up a portable TV in the corner of one of the bedrooms and we all gathered around. The next news flash told us that she had died. It was the most terrible shock, and people all over the country felt the same. We filmed our scenes and everyone went away in stunned silence. I went to Susie's house that afternoon. She had planned a barbecue but everyone stood around the TV looking to see if the newsreaders could give some answers as to why this horrific tragedy had happened. It was such a terribly sad time.

*

Later that year Ricky Tomlinson was at the regional Royal Television Awards in Manchester when he was approached by Caroline Aherne at the bar. Caroline was already well known from her roles in *The Fast Show* and her own show *Mrs Merton*, which had been a huge success. She told Ricky that she was writing a comedy.

'You're going to be my dad, and Sue Johnston's going to be my mum,' she said matter-of-factly.

For a few years after *Brookside* finished Ricky and I hadn't seen each other but we were reunited in a small film, *Preaching to the Perverted*. It was after this that Ricky called me to tell me about his encounter with Caroline. The idea of playing husband and wife again might seem a strange thing to do after being such well-established characters for years, but the Royles were very different to the Grants so we both agreed to do it.

The scripts arrived and were brilliantly funny but so sparse and nothing really seemed to happen – it wasn't like any other TV script I'd seen before. I rang Ricky to see what he thought.

'It'll either be a cult hit or they'll be showing it on the graveyard slot because no one gets it. I don't think there'll be an in between,' he said frankly.

We went to the read-through at Granada. There were heads of production from Granada Studios and from the BBC in London, along with the writing team consisting of Caroline, Craig Cash and Henry Normal. There was a definite feeling of trepidation about the project. Even though everyone seemed to want the next 'original' comedy I think there was an uncertainty about whether this might be a bit too 'original'.

I was very excited when I saw the other actors in the room. There was, of course, Liz Smith who I loved, a very young Ralf Little, Ricky, Caroline, and Craig who played Dave. Also in the cast was Geoff Hughes who played Twiggy but had been known to millions as Eddie Yeats from *Coronation Street*. Kathy Burke was also there reading the part of Cheryl the constantly dieting next-door-neighbour, who was later played by Jessica (Stevenson) Hynes. I was quite star struck by Doreen Keogh who was to play Mary, as she had played Concepta Hewitt in *Coronation Street* when I was younger. We all read the scripts and laughed a lot – a good start for a comedy!

Afterwards, the Granada and BBC heads took the writers to one side and they had a heated discussion while we all sat there wondering what on earth was going on. Eventually Caroline told us to go across to the V&A Hotel over the road from Granada and said she would join us as soon as possible.

She and Craig came over a little later and told us why everything seemed to have ground to a halt. The heads of production were worried that without an audience or music or canned laughter – which had been the norm in comedy – then it would just feel too strange. It hadn't been done before and they were concerned. Caroline said that she and Craig were adamant that it should be very naturalistic, as if we were just watching a family in their living room. They came to an uneasy compromise. We filmed the pilot in a studio as if we were performing in front of an audience.

When it was shot it wasn't at all what Caroline or Craig had wanted. Caroline was so embarrassed by the tape that she buried it in her brother's garden and told me that she would dig it up one day and let us watch it. She never has! Then we waited. The writers reconvened and hurriedly rewrote the episodes, they brought in a new director and we reshot it.

Now it was filmed like a fly-on-the-wall documentary as Caroline had wanted. It felt so completely different to any comedy I could think of. There were no obvious gags, no clever put downs, the pauses were long and natural and the characters were all sitting watching the telly! I remember one direction that specifically jumped out at me when I first read the script: 'They all suck a mint.' Imagine a minute of TV time taken up by a family all sucking on a mint! I loved it, but I had no idea if anyone else would.

I had been a smoker on and off all my life. When we started to film *The Royle Family* I hadn't smoked for years and was very proud of myself for the fact. But Denise and Barbara both smoke like chimneys. At first I did my best to get round it. I would have a cigarette in my hand or put one in my mouth but not light it. Then a little later you would see me stubbing one out in the huge, rarely emptied, ashtray. As the filming wore on I found myself more and more tempted to have a cigarette until eventually I caved in and lit one. That was it – I could never be a casual smoker and I was hooked again!

Caroline really knew how to throw a party. She was very generous and would buy beer and champagne for everyone – and mild for Ricky – on Friday afternoons as the week's filming drew to a close. At the wrap party Caroline and Craig gave out awards to the cast and crew as we all got increasingly sozzled. I was excited to see what my 'Oscar' would be.

Caroline looked at the cast with mock gravitas. 'And the award for the Best Legs in Leggings goes to Sue Johnston!'

I wobbled up to receive my award. I've never been so proud, or so drunk! I'd like to think that I made a fantastic acceptance speech, but I really can't remember.

*

I was given a tape when we finished filming the series. At the time I was staying with Margot and her husband David as I was working in London. I handed it to them and asked them to watch the first episode and then made myself scarce for the evening. I really respected their opinion and so what they thought was very important to me. I returned later, nervous as to what they would say.

Margot opened the door. 'We loved it.'

'Really?' I asked.

'We watched the whole series!' I breathed a sigh of relief. If they liked it then there was every chance that other people would.

The Royle Family aired for the first time on 14 September 1998. No one anticipated the reaction that we received. Overnight it seemed people took the show to their hearts. My family were very impressed. My mother had never been very complimentary about any of the roles I'd played in the past but she loved *The Royle Family*. She called me to tell me the good news. 'I don't care what anyone says, Susan, I think it's good.' A back-handed compliment was better than nothing!

I think for her it was the same as with most working-class people, she could totally relate to it.

My aunty Jean was around at my mum's just after it aired. They had been discussing it and she said, 'I think it's very good but I really don't understand why you have to say "fart", Susan. Can't you have a word with someone about that?'

My mum did take issue with some of the storylines.

'Have you been telling them about my cataracts?' she asked when Norma appeared with a patch on her eye after having her cataracts removed.

'No!' I said honestly. 'I haven't said a word.'

'Well, someone's said something because it was on the programme!'

Mum didn't realise that there were thousands of old ladies going through the same thing as her every week.

Then she called me up to say, 'Nana's got a china cup, I drink out of a china cup!'

Again, I told Mum that other people up and down the country drink out of a china cup; she wasn't unique.

The final straw came when she called and said, 'She was making gravy this week. You've been telling them about me making gravy, haven't you?'

'Mother,' I said, 'you'll be complaining that Nana is breathing just like you next!'

I think she thought I was taking notes when I was with her and feeding them back to Caroline and Craig.

Soon I was being stopped in the street and asked to say, 'What have you had for your tea?' I was interviewed in the Australian press where *The Royle Family* had become a huge hit. Just as the interviewer was about to sign off she said, 'One more thing Sue, can you say "Ahhh" for me?'

So in my best Barbara voice I said 'Ahhh'.

The woman went away delighted.

Caroline was being stopped to say, 'Hiya, Mam!' and Ricky was inundated with requests for a shout of, 'My arse!'

We were on our way to becoming the cult hit that had been fifty per cent of Ricky's prediction. The only person I remember saying they didn't understand what all the fuss was about was David Threlfall, a friend of mine and the actor who would go on to play Frank Gallagher in *Shameless*. I was filming *Sex, Chips and Rock n' Roll* with him when *The Royle Family* came out.

'I'm sorry, Sue,' he said to me one day, 'but I just don't get it.'

'Fair enough,' I thought, 'you can't please all of the people all of the time.'

Very soon a second series was commissioned, but instead of filming in Manchester we were asked to go to Ealing Studios in London. It was great to be back together and to have a hit series under our belts.

The cast all got along brilliantly. The director would stop filming yet we'd all stay on the sofa chatting. Geoff Hughes and Ricky would go off together at lunch time and come back armed with ridiculous power tools that they had no intention of using but that they'd egged each other on to buy. Geoff and Ricky's sense of humour really clicked. Throughout filming *The Royle Family* I felt like I was surrounded by so many funny people that I daren't crack a joke. I felt more comfortable sitting and laughing at their jokes than trying to make them.

There was a really fun and relaxed atmosphere on set. The crew would join in the fun and there was one time when the Royles sang a song with the line, 'she flies like a bird', which was from the theme tune to the Nimble ad. One of the crew had found a loaf of Nimble bread from somewhere and attached it to a boom mike and flew it over our heads as we all tried to concentrate on singing the song without laughing.

The crew also built a naughty corner for us. It started off as just a corner of the set where we would have to stand if we laughed when we shouldn't or forgot our lines but as the series progressed the naughty corner became more and more elaborate until it was an actual prison cell. By the end of the second series we all ended up in it behind bars!

Halfway through the airing of series two I got a call.

'Sue, it's David.' It was David Threlfall. 'I just want to say, I get it now!'

He had watched the second series and enjoyed it so much he had gone back and watched the first. My one dissenter had been won over!

Filming at Ealing studios was something of an honour. Ealing is steeped in TV and film history, and I remember watching the Ealing comedies at home when I was younger.

While we were there I met Michael Barrymore who was working on a series called *Bob Martin* alongside Keith Allen. It was just before the whole scandal broke but I found Michael to be such a warm, funny and lovely man.

You would see a lot of famous faces around the studio, it was great for star spotting. I remember walking to set one day. I had my regulation bobbly jumper and leggings on and my Barbara hair extensions and walking down the stairs in the opposite direction was Patsy Kensit, looking super-glamorous. I said hello to her and scurried off feeling in desperate need of some lipstick and a brush.

Seeing other projects being filmed around you made you feel like you were really part of the wider industry and there was a buzz about the place.

My feet certainly hadn't improved with age and were still a sight of ugliness to behold. They are bent out of shape from constantly shoving them in stilettos when I was younger, scarred from the hot water incident as a child and generally best kept in a darkened shoe. For years I never allowed them to see the light of day. Then I looked at the script one day and the direction said: Barbara takes her slipper off. And I had to say, 'Dave, look at my feet. They're buggered!'

I ran over to Caroline. 'I can't say this!' I said horrified.

'Why, what's up?' she asked.

'My feet. I can't say they're buggered because...well, they are!'

I pulled off my sock to show her what I meant. Surely when she saw the actual state of my feet she wouldn't want them airing on set, never mind going out on national TV.

'They're perfect!' Caroline said.

And so my poor feet made their TV debut without so much as a bit of powder to touch them up.

*

At the end of filming each of the three series we would return home having had a wonderful time together and, without sounding too over the top about it, the love for the show would follow us home. It was great that it chimed with so many people. But *The Royle Family* was not only something that ordinary people enjoyed, critics loved it too, and the show was winning awards left, right and centre. Ricky and I won best performance at the Comedy awards, the show won the comedy BAFTA a number of times, I also was nominated for a BAFTA, and we picked up gongs at nearly every other TV award show there was. It was quite unbelievable and very exciting to go along to these award ceremonies. I would take Joel with me and we'd hobnob with other actors.

On one occasion I had put some 'chicken fillets' into my bra because they were all the rage and I had decided to see what I was missing. I was about to step into a roomful of press after picking up an award when there was a sudden thud at my feet. I looked down to see the offending chicken fillet. I wavered for a few moments, should I bend down and get it and stuff it back in? I checked that no one had seen it was me and then stepped over the offending article and out in front of the press, one boob bigger than the other!

I also worked on other projects in between *The Royle Family*. One was a series called *Duck Patrol* about the

Thames river police. It starred among others Richard Wilson and David Tennant. I'd met Richard before at Labour Party events and I had asked him for his autograph for Joel, who was a huge fan of *One Foot in the Grave*.

My character was the landlady of a pub on the Thames. This was a great role for me and of course I had plenty of experience to draw on having been a barmaid at a pub on the Thames when I was younger. We filmed near Hampton Court, which is one of my favourite places in London, but more personally it is near Shepperton where I had lived a lifetime ago with Neil's mother Peggy. I felt very nostalgic revisiting these old haunts. I went to the Red Lion pub where I had worked and been advised about the nose job. The place had changed so much. I couldn't help but think about my life back then and how things had turned out for me. I had been such a lost soul when I had lived with Peggy and now here I was doing the job I had hoped I would be doing, with my son off at college. I felt that I had come quite some way.

Richard Wilson had played Victor Meldrew brilliantly, and the character's name had become a byword for late middle-aged grumpiness. But more than that, the expression 'I don't believe it' had become so synonymous with Meldrew that Richard was to be for ever associated with it. I quickly grew to recognise the signs that he was about to be asked for his favourite line. You would see that someone had spotted him. They would then head over and say, 'It's you, isn't it?'

Richard would politely nod and confirm that yes, it was him.

'Go on then, say it,' they would demand, waiting for Richard to say his infamous line. Poor Richard.

One day Richard and David, who both were playing river policemen, were filming a scene in a speedboat on the Thames. Richard had a police uniform on with a peaked police cap pulled down over his eyes. He was sitting down low in the boat behind the windscreen. How anyone could have recognised him without actually sitting next to him I have no idea. The director shouted 'action' and as the camera rolled a barge passed in the background. On board was a group of men who were clearly on a stag do. Just as Richard was about to begin speaking his lines, the lads on the boat shouted in unison, 'I don't believe it!' Poor Richard, how on earth they knew it was him I have no idea!

*

In 2000 we filmed the third and final series of *The Royle Family*. The final episode was the Christmas special where it's Baby David's first birthday and we all sit down to Christmas dinner together. Jim gets the best Christmas present anyone could ever have bought him: Sky TV!

After *The Royle Family* ended, Craig went on to make *Early Doors* and Caroline moved to Australia for a time.

But we all stayed in touch and any time I meet up with any of them it really does feel like I'm meeting up with family. In fact, Caroline calls me her second mum. They say all good things must come to an end but on this occasion I wished it didn't have to. I genuinely loved being Barbara Royle.

Chapter Eighteen

I WAS AT the National Theatre performing in *The Mysteries* and staying with my friend Anna Keaveney and her partner Mark when I was offered a pilot in a new TV drama. It followed a police team who investigate murders that had been closed years before, or 'cold cases'. They were charged with using the latest advances in DNA and criminal profiling to reopen these cases and solve the crime. At that time, the police had only been using these new scientific advances on cold cases for a few years so to see it on TV was something very new.

The character I was to play was called Grace Foley and the new show was *Waking the Dead*. I was very excited because Trevor Eve was to star in the main role of Peter Boyd. I had never met him, but I knew him to be a wonderful actor. Holly Aird, Will Johnson and Claire Goose were all in the cast too. I was drawn to the part because the concept was so interesting and new.

I met the woman whom my character was based on. She was a psychological profiler for the Metropolitan Police, and the minute I met her I knew how to play this character. She was warm and friendly and extremely down to earth. She was also very unruffled. I wanted to bring this calmness and confidence to Grace. I also wanted her to appear as if she had a life outside of work, and that she had lived an interesting life.

In the pilot a lot of the action took place in the less than glamorous location of a landfill site in South-East London. It was pretty grim and stank to high heaven, and we were all given protective clothing to wear. When it was time to film the actors were told to hand over their protective clothing and we disrobed and stood knee deep in muck while the crew all looked on through their white paper suits.

One of the first scenes I filmed with Trevor was of us driving over the site in a 4x4. As we had only just met we were still very much at the pleasantries stage. But as soon as Trevor put his foot on the pedal the pleasantries went out of the window. He shot off at a hundred miles an hour while I clung on like grim death. He drove like a lunatic! When we finished the scene I said, 'Did you think you were on *Top Gear*?' to which he just shrugged, suggesting that it might be something I'd just have to get used to. A few years later Trevor would go on *Top Gear* and fly round the track, swearing and destroying a wheel into the bargain: he clocked a great time though. Looking back I think I got off quite lightly!

A few days later we were filming a scene on the South Bank in London. I had to run across the concourse in heels. As I set off running one leg went one way and the other went the other. I heard a pop and then suddenly was in absolute agony. I was taken to hospital and informed that I had snapped my hamstring. I was bandaged up and had to stay in overnight.

But not only did I have to finish off filming the pilot for *Waking the Dead*, I had to continue performing in *The Mysteries*. In that role I had to sing and dance and generally jig around on an out-of-action leg. The director at the National decided to work around my damaged leg and so I was able to be onstage, and some one else danced for me. Back on *Waking the Dead*, because of some insurance clause, I had to be chaperoned. I was literally lifted from a wheelchair to wherever the action was taking place and I went from being very animated to sitting behind a desk for the last days of filming.

During the pilot we really gelled as a team and there was such enthusiasm and passion from Trevor for the role which the rest of us found terribly infectious. When we were told that the BBC wanted to make the series I was really happy to be going to work with this great bunch of people.

From the beginning I realised that working on *Waking the Dead* wasn't going to be an easy ride but it was all the better for being challenging. Trevor is a perfectionist and he would go over the scripts time and again, asking that things be changed if he thought they could be improved. My natural inclination is to not cause a fuss but Trevor was constantly striving to make the show the best that it could be. It took time to have the confidence to do this but I quickly learned to be confident about my character Grace.

One thing that never seemed to get any easier was managing to say the psychology terms that Grace had to pronounce. I would sit in her office and look around at these huge tomes and think, Grace has read all of these books!

One day I stared at the script – 'countertransference', 'diathesis stress hypothesis' and 'Electra complex' all stared back at me. I stumbled across the lines like a child trying to get out a particularly difficult tongue twister.

'Come on, Sue!' the director David Thacker said. 'It's got to trip off the tongue! Grace says these things every day.'

'Diathesis stress hypothesis,' I stuttered. I really wasn't sounding particularly confident.

'Trip it off the tongue, trip, trip, trip!'

I stuttered a couple more times and then just started laughing and had to start again.

In the end I went away and learned the lines, and eventually I managed to trip them off the tongue for the camera but I needed a large glass of wine when I was finished. I would get the scripts and begin learning the lines straight away, scared to death that I was going to come unstuck with the unfamiliar terms.

Having said that I didn't have it as tough as poor old

Tara Fitzgerald. When she joined the show in 2006, I was delighted to be working with Tara again. We had worked together on *Brassed Off* and now she came in to play Eve Lockhart the forensic pathologist. Tara would have reams of medical terms to recite and any time she stumbled over the lines we would all stand around off camera, giggling, while she stood trying to remain composed but wanting to throttle us all!

Having played Barbara Royle for three years, to play a role like Grace was a big change and a challenge which I relished. I was always very proud to be able to play Grace and people were always very complimentary. I was fifty-six when I was first cast as Grace and it could quite easily have gone to a younger woman or even a man. But Barbara Machin who created the series was adamant that she should be a mature woman. All of the female characters in *Waking the Dead* were strong and brilliantly drawn.

I always loved the relationship between Boyd and Grace. There was never any element of romance but they were very close and knew one another extremely well. They often fell out and he could be dismissive and disrespectful to some of her ideas, but on the whole they were a team. The antagonism between the two was a great way of creating drama and helped to lift the facts off the page.

We would perform scenes where Trevor and I would chat in the office together. Over time the writers allowed us to ad-lib them as they trusted us to know what the two characters would talk about. One scene I remember well was when Trevor and I were talking. Trevor suggested to the director that he should be doing something in the scene so he suggested he wash his feet. There is something quite personal about someone getting their size tens out and scrubbing them in front of a colleague and I think it said a huge amount about how relaxed the two characters were with each other without any words being exchanged.

I was so pleased that *Waking the Dead* went on to run for ten series. All of the crew who worked on it were absolutely fantastic. We all had a great time working together. I think that the success of the show was down to the chemistry of the team, and that the scripts were brilliant and credited the audience with the intelligence they deserved.

*

During one of the breaks in filming *Waking the Dead* I was in *The Play What I Wrote*, a comical look at the comedy duo Morecambe and Wise and the relationship between comedy duos in general. We started at the Liverpool Playhouse and went on to Wyndham's Theatre in London. In the second half of the play a guest artist would appear to star in 'the play what I wrote'.

We did a special performance for the Prince's Trust and I was delighted when Kylie Minogue agreed to be the guest star. She was great fun, very down to earth and sweet. Afterwards I arrived at the party to see her sitting with Dawn French and Jennifer Saunders. It was before *Jam and Jerusalem*, which I would work with them on. Dawn's face dropped when she saw me. She looked horrified; I wondered what I had done.

'What?' I asked.

'We've just spent all day being you,' Dawn replied.

'Being me?' I exclaimed. I couldn't think what she could mean.

'We're doing *Waking the Dead* for the Christmas Special,' she explained. 'I'm you and Jennifer's Boyd.'

I laughed, extremely flattered. I have to say that, in my opinion, to have French and Saunders perform a skit of your show means you've arrived.

'Right,' I said, sitting down next to them. 'Do you want some tips?'

I let them into a few trade secrets, one of which was that when we remove our glasses and put them back on again, it's usually because we were looking at a script. When the sketch came out they had us putting on and taking off the glasses almost constantly throughout.

The next time I would meet Jennifer would be by pure coincidence but it would be the start of a new friendship.

*

Susie and I had gathered a group of us together to stay in a pub in Devon for the New Year. My cousin David had recommended the pub-cum-B&B and Susie and I had discovered it for ourselves the previous summer. It was on the moors with roaring log fires – picture perfect. My friend Anna Keaveney was meant to be coming with us, but she had sadly passed away after a hard battle with lung cancer in November of that year, 2004. I was very saddened by her death and she was, and is, sorely missed. I was very pleased, though, that her partner Mark was able to come.

On New Year's Eve, I got dolled up and headed to the bar to meet with my friends and family. As I was sitting there, who should be in a corner of the bar with her husband Ade and their children but Jennifer Saunders. It turned out that the landlord was Jennifer's brother.

I got a drink and went to sit with them, and Jennifer said, 'I'm writing a series for you, Sue.'

I was delighted. I loved *French and Saunders* and *Absolutely Fabulous* and I was thrilled with the idea of being in Jennifer's next show.

'And,' she went on, 'the woman I'm basing it on is over here, come and meet her.' She took me over to meet her friend Cindy and we had a good chat. And this is how I first heard about *Jam and Jerusalem*.

The evening descended into drunken debauchery and we all had a marvellous time, playing parlour games that none of us could quite keep up with and chatting into the wee small hours.

I awoke the next day with a sore head and then returned to London hoping that I would hear from

Jennifer but putting it to the back of my mind for the time being. Eventually, months later, my agent rang to say that a script had arrived. I loved it and was delighted to hear who else was going to be in the cast. Among them was my friend Maggie Steed who I had known since the early seventies.

When I arrived in Devon to begin filming it was to discover that my home for the next couple of months would be Jennifer's brother's pub. My overriding memory of my time on *Jam and Jerusalem* was how much we laughed. Again, like on *The Royle Family*, I was surrounded by funny people. It was great to be an audience with this many fantastic performers. Jennifer and I had a great rivalry. She is a massive Manchester United fan and of course I am Liverpool through and through.

We would have great evenings out after filming and I remember one evening sitting in the pub getting merrily merry when I got chatting to one of the supporting artists. He was very friendly and asked me if I'd ever considered a tattoo. I hadn't, I told him, but now that he mentioned it...

So I sat with him for the rest of the night, carefully planning what my tattoo was going to look like, I was going to mark my dedication to Liverpool for life. I stopped short of suggesting Stevey Gerrard's head and decided on a simple Liver Bird, the symbol of the club.

The following day I awoke with a hangover and when I arrived on set the tattooist was there, ready for me with all his equipment. I looked at him in horror. I had to politely tell him that I wouldn't be requiring a tattoo after all.

I really loved the camaraderie on *Jam and Jerusalem*, of working with this great gang of women. It was a very supportive environment and one in which I felt I could share what was on my mind with the girls. Which was something I became very thankful of.

Chapter Nineteen

I T WAS AROUND this time that I noticed a real decline in my mother. Things had been going downhill for the past few years but now it was getting serious. My mum had, of course, always been a forceful character and that extended to telling me her opinion of old people's homes.

'You're not putting me in a home!' she had told me on numerous occasions.

So when the strong, forthright, no-nonsense woman I had grown up with began to be beset by health problems, I, at first, tried to care for her myself.

Mum had always been so well turned out that even now, at ninety, she was still determined to look after herself and look the best she could. I would head home at the weekend to take care of her.

I arrived home one weekend from filming *Jam and Jerusalem* and I waited in the sitting room while she was getting ready; she refused any help, she was too proud. It had begun to take my mother longer and longer to perform her ablutions. Eventually I got up and went to investigate what was going on.

'Mother, what are you doing?' I asked, standing outside the bathroom door.

'I'm getting a wash,' she snapped back. 'What d'you think I'm doing? Flying a kite?'

She was having a full body wash while standing by the sink. The idea that she might smell petrified her, but she had stopped having a bath some time ago for fear of having a fall. And she wouldn't have a shower because she didn't trust them. 'Too much like a watering can.'

After what seemed like an eternity she eventually emerged, dressed immaculately with her pearls and red lipstick on.

Over the past few years her respiratory problems had worsened. She had also begun to suffer falls that were becoming increasingly severe. I had to admit that she was a danger to herself, doing things like leaving the gas on and not realising she had. Her mind was becoming affected by dementia; one day she would be fine, the next she would be imagining things. She began to have an on-going hallucination about a young boy who lived on the roof whom she could see through the window.

Sometimes I arrived to find her particularly agitated. For instance, one day she was very concerned.

'He's getting wet,' she said anxiously.

I sat down in the chair next to her. 'Who?' I asked.

'The boy on the roof. It's raining and no one's brought him in, poor love. He's feeding them birds but who's feeding him?' She looked worried. 'I'm not sure he's looked after,' Mum added, straining her neck to look at the roof outside.

I strained my neck too, knowing full well that there was no one there. After a good while of listening to my mother's tales, I headed into the kitchen to make a cup of tea. On my return she looked much happier.

'Next door have put a telly in the top room for him so he can watch his programmes,' she said, satisfied.

'That's nice of them, isn't it?' I said agreeably, supping my tea.

We used to have these conversations over and over again. At times I did feel like I was going doolally myself but I didn't want to burst my mother's bubble. The doctor said it would frighten her if she were to be confronted with the truth when she was so convinced of what she imagined.

One day, one of my uncles came to visit. My mother was happily telling him all about the boy on the roof when he snapped at her, pulling back the curtains and gesticulating out of the window. 'For God's sake, Margaret, there's no one there!'

My mother's face crumpled. She looked distraught and went very quiet. When my uncle had gone she became tearful and said to me, 'They think I'm mad, don't they?'

I hated seeing her like this, upset and frightened. In cases like this it was far better to pretend that what she imagined was actually happening.

But sometimes I had to disillusion her for her own

good. She would call me in the middle of the night, confused and distressed. She would have fallen asleep and then awake not knowing what time it was, got dressed, put on the TV and fallen asleep again in front of it. Whatever was on the TV so late at night would form the backbone to her confused state.

Once, the phone began to ring at two o'clock in the morning. I jumped out of bed. 'Hello!' I shouted into the receiver.

Although I knew at the back of my mind that it would be my mother, there was always the fear that it was someone else ringing because something had happened to her, if she'd managed to get out of the house and was wandering around, or had a fall, or something even worse.

'Susan!' she shouted hysterically. 'Your leg! What's happened to your leg?'

'Nothing, Mum,' I reassured her. 'My leg is fine.'

'It's not. It's on the telly now and it's gashed open. There's blood everywhere.'

'Mum, I'm looking at both of my legs and honestly, they're fine.'

'It's hanging off!'

'It isn't, Mum!'

'Have they stopped the bleeding?'

'There isn't any bleeding, Mum, honestly.'

'But it's on the telly, Susan, I can see it.'

Mum sounded so utterly distraught that I was

desperate to calm her down. Knowing that there was little I could do to allay her fears from two hundred miles away, I put the phone to my legs, stamped on the floor several times and shouted, 'Look, I'm fine, Mother, two legs, in perfect working order.'

There was silence on the other end of the phone as Mum tried to take this in. Then she said quietly, 'Oh well, okay. If you're sure.'

'I'm sure, Mum. Try to get some sleep.'

She eventually believed me and went back to bed. These incidents were so distressing for her because she believed in the reality of them. And it took a lot of reassurance to convince her everything was all right and being so far away made this difficult to give.

Throughout my mother's dementia she would see members of the family that had long since died and inform me that they had just been in to visit. But she only ever imagined that she had seen my father once. I arrived one day to find her sitting quietly, looking very displeased.

'You all right, Mum?' I asked.

She nodded towards the bedroom. 'He's in there, sulking.'

'Who is?' I asked.

'Your father,' she said, adamantly. 'I'm not going in there while he's in there.'

I went into the bedroom and came back out again. 'It's all right, Mum, he's gone,' I said, and after that she never claimed to have seen my dad. Of course she would talk about him and refer back to things that they had done together but she never imagined she'd seen him again.

*

The guilt that I used to feel leaving Joel as a boy when I went to work was now replaced with the guilt of working while my mother was ill. Throughout this time I soldiered on, trying to look after her myself and work at the same time. I was living life on an ad hoc basis, with no time for myself, just work and spending time looking after my mother. My aunty Jean and other members of my family were brilliant and mucked in constantly and Susie was always on the other end of the phone ready to help out with my mother while I was away working. My family and Susie lived nearby and were an absolute godsend.

My mother, on the other hand, didn't quite see things the way that I did. While everyone else was busy making sure that she was looked after, she made her feelings quite clear on the subject of me being away working half the week. I should give up work and move back to Warrington to look after her. She wanted me near. 'Why couldn't you have married a plumber?' she would still ask with great disappointment.

I might have had the same thought myself on the few occasions that my shower leaked or I couldn't find the stopcock but I didn't necessarily see it as an essential component of a fulfilled life!

One day I arrived at my mother's, laden down with shopping bags, and set about stocking the fridge. She must have felt that she had exhausted the 'Why couldn't you have married a plumber?' line of attack so instead she said, 'I wish you'd never had an education!'

I took a deep breath, bit my tongue and continued stocking the fridge. I didn't think that going into the whys and wherefores of my education would be particularly constructive so I took the eggs out of the box and put them into the fridge compartment instead, trying not to smash them in frustration.

Of course, my mother's disappointment in me was nothing new – she'd been saying things like this all my life – but it was frustrating. I was working flat out, flying up the motorway any time I had a day off, only to be greeted with constant criticism.

I knew that I couldn't move back home and become my mother's full-time carer, although the guilt often saw me toy with the idea. My friends and family were quite clear with me, they knew that I would go stir crazy if I did this, and I would resent my mother for forcing my hand. They also knew that my mother was definitely wearing her rose-tinted spectacles. If I had been around her twenty-four hours a day, not only would I have gone potty, I would have driven her to distraction too.

For the first few years of her decline I gave her lots of

options rather than being firm with her and making the decision I thought was right. A good example of this was the Meals on Wheels episode. My mother was adamant she wasn't having Meals on Wheels. 'Who do you think I am?' she would snap.

Whether she felt that cooking her own food was one of the last vestiges of independence that she wasn't willing to forgo or it simply was plain snobbery I'm not quite sure. So for over four years, every week I would drive from London to Warrington, go to a Marks & Spencer food hall – it had to be M&S, not Morrison's or Tesco, thank you very much! – and stock her fridge full of food so that she could cook for herself. The idea of this seems like such a short-term solution to a long-term problem now that I think about it, a four-hundred-mile round trip to take my mother shopping, every week! But at the time it felt like the only option. I was literally running up and down the country to keep my mother happy.

I suppose I'd had a lifetime of trying to keep the peace, always going out of my way to not offend my mother. On a more basic level, of course, I wanted to know that she was getting regular good food. In the end I had to put my foot down and with a heavy heart I ordered in Meals on Wheels. She was adamant she would only have three meals to begin with and she was very sniffy about the food at first. 'There's no salt in it!' she declared, insisting the food was tasteless and bland.

'Well, put some salt on it, then!' I said in exasperation. It might not be the healthiest thing but it was a simple pleasure and meant that she stopped complaining about her Meals on Wheels delivery and started to enjoy them.

She soon realised that the food she was being brought was good, home-cooked food, so she allowed me to order in more meals for her. And eventually she forged a relationship with the man that delivered the meals, a man from Liverpool with a great sense of humour whom Mum always hugely looked forward to seeing. One of the advantages of having Meals on Wheels was that they would just leave them for you, you didn't have to be in. But Mum always wanted to make sure she was back so she could have a bit of banter with her new friend. Something that she had resisted for so long became one of the highlights of her day.

There were regular battles like this. She refused to have a wheelchair for a long time, insisting on getting about with a Zimmer frame with wheels on. I understood that accepting that she would be better off in a wheelchair was a huge step for her so I didn't push it, but I gently tried to urge her to think about it. When she finally relented she realised I could push her around in it, like the Queen Mother, which suited her just fine! It meant for me that we could get out and about together a bit more and see more of the world without a constant battle over her waning independence. We would go to the park, to the garden centre (somewhere my mother loved to visit 'for a look'), to get a cup of coffee and a cake and of course we could go to Marks together too.

As my mother's health began to get worse, I was receiving constant worried phone calls at work. Yet I was still trying to make this impossible situation work. When she had a fall that saw her hospitalised again I knew that I had to do something but I really didn't want to go against her wishes. Meanwhile, she was constantly anxious and imagining things. I decided that I needed to get some outside carers in to help with my mother. Mum was extremely truculent when presented with these women invading her space, as she saw it.

I would no sooner be through the door than Mum would grab me and whisper conspiratorially. 'Them nurses,' she hissed referring to her carers, 'they're taking my tea bags. They stick them in their pockets and go out with them.'

I would tell her that I didn't think that was the case.

'They do!' she would protest getting upset. 'You don't know what it's like because you're not here to see it.'

I managed to talk my mum round and convince her that the carers were a good thing, but she still kept an eye on her PG Tips.

*

A few months earlier I had received a call from Caroline Aherne. I thought that she was calling up for a chat but she said, 'Sue, I'm going to do another *Royle Family*, are you in?'

She explained that she had been to her grandmother's funeral in Ireland and it had made her think that she wanted to do another *Royle Family*. The one thing she would be really sad about was to kill Nana off but if we were coming back after six years then it had to be for something big.

Meeting up with everyone again was fantastic. Six years on, Anthony was all grown up and we were all back in the house with Nana living in the living room. Caroline had written in the script that Nana picks up a magnifying glass and we see her big magnified eye through it, something she had seen her own grandmother do. I was in hysterics watching Liz do this and it still makes me smile now thinking about it.

It was great to all be back together but while we were filming I was leaving the set and heading straight to see Mum. There is a scene in the episode where Jim puts down a laminate floor. I'm not in it because I had been called to the hospital. After we filmed the scenes by Nana's bedside as she is dying, I again had to head straight to my mum's bedside in the hospital. It was very sad for me. Liz reminded me of my mother. In her later years Mum had snow-white hair like the wig Liz wore as Nana, and looked quite like her. But it was more than that.

When the 'Queen of Sheba' episode aired later that year I didn't tell my mother that it was on. It would have been too upsetting for her, and for me. She identified with Nana and to see her die would have shocked her.

Everyone seemed pleased that *The Royle Family* had returned and with such a heart-rending story. I was just very sad for Liz. She loved the Royles, we really were a family for her. Since then we have made three Christmas specials and Liz has been sadly missed by everyone.

*

Other people had begun pointing out to me how ridiculous this situation was with me flying up to be with Mum whenever I had a free moment. Aunty Jean took me in hand one day.

Mum was having a doze in her chair and Jean nodded to the garden, so we both went outside. Jean was thoughtful for a moment, then she said, 'Susan, love, you can't go on like this.'

I was on the verge of tears. She was right, of course, but hearing it said out loud made me very upset. I felt slightly underhand, out here in the garden discussing my mother's life when she was only a few feet away.

'I'm going to move home and look after her myself,' I said again, feeling that this was definitely the only option.

Jean shook her head. 'Don't be silly,' she said gently. 'How would you live?'

'Well, I'll find a job,' I replied.

'Where? What else can you do?'

She had a point. I'm not sure there was much call at Warrington job centre for someone who could recite Pinter. I shrugged my shoulders, fighting back tears.

'Susan, if you moved back you'd want to kill your mother within five minutes and she'd want to kill you,' Jean reasoned with me. 'It's madness. You need proper help. Not me, not anyone else we know. Real help from people who know what they're doing.'

I looked at my aunty Jean and nodded. I couldn't move back home, it was nonsense. I needed to keep working and mum needed full-time care. But as with everything with my mum it took me a long time and a number of changes in my mother's condition to implement what Jean and I had discussed.

I seriously considered bringing her to live with me, but Joel was living with me at the time. He cared very much for my mother, but I knew that when I was away with work the burden of care would naturally default to Joel and I didn't want to shoulder him with this responsibility.

Where my mother lived in Warrington was a great community, with lovely neighbours and people who looked out for her. I felt that if she was to go into a care home it must feel like this. So I began to notice care homes, seeing if they fitted in with the picture in my head of what a care home for my mother should be. Whenever we were out for a drive or a meal I would spot them, having never noticed them before – in the same way when you get a new car you suddenly see that make and model everywhere. I'd think, did they look inviting, did they have a sign half hanging off, unloved and uncared for which immediately made me think 'like my mother would be if she went there!'

One day I was driving through the lovely village of Grappenhall on the outskirts of Warrington when I spotted a care home that looked perfect. It was in a lovely position, just by the side of the canal in a semi-rural setting. There were two pubs in the cobbled square, which I thought would be handy for people visiting my mother – not that I'm saying she drove everyone to drink but it was nice for people to go for a catch-up after they'd visited. I could imagine us going for walks along the canal. There was a wonderful old church next door; in fact, the old people's home had formerly been the rectory. It looked so inviting that I was a bit worried about going in because I thought it might be a disappointment. I'd been to retirement homes before, when I'd visited other elderly relatives, places that were a dreaded cliché of old people's homes: they weren't clean, smelled of urine and were like glorified prisons. After such a promising start from the outside I dreaded this place being the same.

As I walked in a lovely nurse came over and introduced herself and was so warm and welcoming that I felt immediately at ease. She was the sister and introduced herself as Theresa. She said that she understood that the decision I was trying to make was an extremely difficult one. She explained that everyone who came through the door on behalf of their elderly parents had the same choice to make after coming to the same impasse in their lives. It feels like a very solitary decision to make when you're the one having to do it.

She showed me around and the staff all seemed very jolly and happy to work there. There were some bits of my first trip around the home that were how I had feared it to be – some old people were sitting in the TV room staring into space or sleeping – but of course this came with the territory. The important thing to me was the feeling of industry around the place. There were activities, people were here to interact with the residents and make their days interesting. There were some playing cards – which I knew my mother would love as she was a big fan of canasta. There was occupational therapy taking place and there was a group of old ladies having their hair done because, it transpired, the owner was a hairdresser and this was one of the weekly treats. Also I was told that they gave manicures on a regular basis. I couldn't help thinking that my mother would love that, being pampered every week. Food was cooked fresh on the premises. The notice board was full of ongoing activities and photographs of trips and outings that the residents had been on. I would recommend to anyone looking at a prospective home to check out the notice boards and see what regular activities there are.

I was then shown the bedrooms and they were all bright and spacious and the whole place was light and airy. There was no gloom and doom, or sense of God's Waiting Room about this place. Outside the gardens were green and well kept and I could imagine my mother sitting out there on a summer's day. The area too was somewhere that I knew my mother would be happy with if she could ever be happy about the idea of going into a care home. Grappenhall was near Stockton Heath, 'the posh part of Warrington'. When I was younger my aunty Millie had a friend who they thought was posh and lived in Stockton Heath. I think maybe subconsciously this notion that my mother should go somewhere she deemed well heeled led me to drive around the area. After my look around the care home that day, I came away feeling lighter. If my mother could go somewhere like this, then I would feel a lot happier that she was well cared for. At the time though, it still wasn't a decision I was willing to make on my mother's behalf.

Within weeks of this, however, my mother was in hospital with another bout of illness. The doctor was a constant visitor to her bedside. My mother was on a respirator most of the day and her dementia was getting completely out of control.

It was clear now that she was becoming a danger to herself, and the nurses at the hospital tried to impress upon me the need for more consistent long-term care: my mother could no longer look after herself. I was taken to one side and told that they would not sign her out unless she had somewhere to go where she had night-time care. I called the home in Grappenhall and asked if there were any places available. There was, in a shared room. I was just relieved that they had a place. So I reluctantly told her about the home. I said that it was somewhere she could go to convalesce.

As it happens, this turn of phrase appealed to my mother. She had been ill with respiratory problems all her life, and after her severe bout of pneumonia when she was in her forties she had been to a convalescence home in North Wales to recover. She had quite enjoyed the genteel notion of 'convalescence'; there was something about the ritual surrounding that word that seemed to really appeal to her. She had been a hypochondriac for years and I think that the idea that she was being looked after post-illness was tantamount to her being able to say, 'See, I told you I was ill!'

So she went from hospital to the care home. I told her that she could go home when she was ready, but I could see that she liked it from the day she moved in. She shared a room with another lady at first so there wasn't much space to make the place her own. I asked her then if she would like some artificial flowers and pictures. I wanted to make the place more homely for her, but she couldn't have real flowers due to her asthma. When she moved to her single room I suggested that I should bring more of her own things in. I wanted to be gentle in this as I didn't want her thinking she would never see her own house again. It was all very gradual, just a few bits brought in at a time. Making sure she was settled was most important.

My mother always kept an eye on what was going on back at her house. One day I came in to find her sitting there in her best clothes, ready for the off. 'I want to go home, I can't stand all these old people!' she hissed, looking round to make sure that none of the 'old people' had heard her.

'You can't go home, Mum,' I said, thinking on my feet. 'The doctor needs to see you first before you go anywhere and he's not around at the moment.' I sat down next to her. 'What's the rush to go home?' I asked.

'It's my home, I can go there if I want, can't I?' She fixed her eyes on me. 'You haven't sold it have you?' As if all of this was a Machiavellian plot on my part to sell her two-bed bungalow and pocket the riches.

I explained that she couldn't go home because she wasn't well enough.

After this whenever Mum mentioned her house I was always keen to reassure her that her house was still there for her to return to whenever she wished. It often felt like dealing with a child in that I was always negotiating, always giving hope without promising something I couldn't deliver on. She never did go back, and as time passed she asked for more and more of her things, and made a real home for herself in the care home. But always in the knowledge that she could return to her own house any time she wished.

Once in the care home her imaginings became less distressing, or at least there was always someone there to hold her hand and try to help her make sense of what she was thinking. But at the same time, what was going on in her head seemed to get increasingly fanciful. The nurses in the care home would wait to tell me what my mother had come up with that week. I arrived one morning to see my mother, sitting in her chair.

'Have you brought him?' she asked.

'Brought who?' I replied.

'Well, I hope you have because they're all waiting for you,' she said, nodding through to where the nurses were.

I was confused. 'Who am I meant to have with me, Mum?' I asked.

'Your boyfriend,' she said. 'That one.' My mother gesticulated at the TV; Wimbledon was on.

I went in search of one of the nurses and found Theresa. 'We've all been hearing about you,' she said with a grin. 'You've been having it away with Rafa Nadal for the past six months, according to your mother.'

Theresa said that my mother would sit watching the tennis waxing lyrical to her and her colleagues about how her sixty-three-year-old daughter was stepping out with the twenty-two-year-old tennis player.

This wasn't the first time that she had me linked to a sporting superstar. She would tell my family when they went to visit that I was pregnant. No mean feat for someone in their early sixties, but not only was I pregnant, I was pregnant with David Beckham's child, who just so happened to be living next door according to my mother. My family thought this was hilarious and would always have something to say about this. 'Has the baby been born yet, Sue? It'd better get a wriggle on, it's been in there two years,' and 'Wait till the papers find out, Sue…', 'What will Victoria say?' At least in Mother's imagination my choice of men was easy on the eye!

I did point out to my mother that I was well past the age where women usually fell pregnant. 'Well,' she said looking at me like I'd been up to something she disapproved of, 'I know they can do things these days.'

When I was visiting my mother I tried to think of things to bring with me that she would like, but the things that she enjoyed were limited. She wasn't a book person; in fact, I rarely saw her read so much as a magazine, unlike me. I love books, and not just reading them, I love owning them, some might say hoarding them – I can never throw a book away and always feel it has to go to a good home or stay on my shelf. In fact, my mother once commented to my friend Margot, 'Our Susan would rather read a book than clean her house,' as if this was the ultimate besmirchment of my character. My mother would much rather put the vac round.

So in order to keep my mother entertained I would talk to her or bring things in to prompt her to chat. When Mother was in a genial mood she liked to talk about the past. When she was fed up it wasn't such a good idea as she could become quite maudlin. I would gauge how she was feeling and would often bring in old photographs for her to look at if I felt she was up to seeing them. She would remember everybody and these old pictures would open up a wealth of stories and memories for her. It was nice for me, too, to hear these stories. We often found it hard to simply chat when we were in one another's company, we soon ran out of things to say, but having these photos as a memory aid meant that my mother had lots to talk about and I was happy to listen.

One thing my mother was happy to impart, right up until her final breath, was her opinion of others. The nurses would be in chatting to her, 'Are you all right, Margaret?'

'Yes, love, thank you. You've been very good,' Mum would say smiling and then as if to reiterate how good she had been, she'd add, 'She's been very good, Susan. Can't do enough for me.' Mum would then watch the nurse leave. The minute the door was shut my mother's vinegar face would form and she'd tell me in no uncertain terms, 'I can't stand her!'

'Why?' I'd ask, horrified.

'She gets on my nerves,' she'd say, with no further explanation.

She could be so charming to your face, my mother, but God help you if you turned your back!

Chapter Twenty

AUNTY MILLIE WAS everyone's favourite aunt, I loved her dearly. She was the sister closest in age to my mum. She was beautiful and bubbly and she and Mum were very close and shared a special bond. She was staying in Woking with my cousin David and his wife Ali, when Ali discovered blood on some of Millie's clothes. It transpired that Millie had been hiding the fact that she had breast cancer. She must have been worried sick but had never told anyone of her concerns. Millie was the opposite to my mother. Where Mum was happy to tell everyone about every ailment, whether real or imagined, Aunty Millie had never taken a pill or seen a doctor. One of my favourite stories involves Millie. I was filming *My Uncle Silas* with Albert Finney, and David and Ali brought Millie along to the set. I knew they'd be delighted to meet this legendary actor. I was saying something about being tired when Millie looked at Albert and piped up, 'Wait till she gets to our age, eh, Albert?'

'How old do you think I am, Millie?' Albert laughed.

Millie shrugged, the same age as her evidently. Albert

is seven years my senior so would have been in his sixties; Millie was ninety at the time!

David and Ali took Millie to hospital but she didn't want to go. Once she was examined and the test results came back they discovered that it was too late to do anything about the cancer. All that they could do was care for her.

I knew that I had to tell my mother. There were lots of things that I kept from Mum, that I thought she would only worry about, especially when she was older, but at any age I didn't want her to find out that Millie had died when she had the opportunity to see her one last time.

I told Mum and she immediately wanted to see her sister. The funny thing about mum being a hypochondriac and worrier was that when she was actually faced with something real and important, like her sister dying, she took it on the chin and became very practical, even now that she was very elderly.

I packed for the trip, making sure that we had provisions for the drive down. My mother wasn't a great traveller by this time and we couldn't go anywhere without a good supply of Tena Lady, so Woking was going to be a bit of a challenge! I had to get my mother and her wheelchair in and out of the car but there was no complaining from her, she was in good spirits all the way there.

We arrived at David and Ali's and they were waiting to help me get my mother and her wheelchair out of the car.

I gave them both a hug; it was a very emotional occasion for all of us.

I had brought Mum's walking frame on wheels and Mum shuffled into the conservatory where Millie was sitting. Millie had very little sight left now, her eyes had been failing for some time.

'Is that you, Margaret?' Millie asked.

'Yes, Millie,' my mother said, moving towards her. Mum began to cry, it was heartbreaking to watch. I went over and helped Mum sit down next to her sister. Mum took Millie's hand and they sat there for a moment, together. After a little while they began to chat and it was like old times: they reminisced and laughed, and it really was the most amazing and moving thing to witness, the love that these two old ladies had for one another.

My aunty Millie became tired very quickly and after an hour she needed to sleep and so she and my mother said goodbye. They were both very upset, as were David, Ali and I.

My mother and I drove to my London flat. I had bought it so that I had a base in London while working on *Waking the Dead*. It was a ground-floor flat in an Edwardian terraced house. My mother loved it. 'It's a bit like a bungalow, Susan, isn't it?' she had said, impressed that everything was on one floor and that we had access to the garden. We went to bed early that night after such an emotional day.

The next morning I had set the table and I woke my

mother up and brought her through. There was a place set for each of us and I had made a hearty breakfast. As I placed the food in front of my mother she took her napkin and smoothed it out over her knee and then picked up the salt cellar and looked thoughtful. After a few moments she said, 'You do do things nicely, don't you, Susan?' Then she put some salt on her breakfast and began to eat.

She had no idea how much that one little line of praise meant to me. I suppose I had always yearned for my mother's approval, which wasn't something that was readily given. But it was little moments like this with my mother, little jewels of memory that I now treasure. The fact that they were infrequent makes them more poignant.

We drove back north; the journey was long and had many toilet stops but it had been worth it for Mum to see her sister one last time. Aunty Millie died a month later.

*

My mother had her ninety-second birthday in the grounds of the home. It was July 2007. It had been a beautiful sunny day and she, who was always smartly turned out, looked lovely in her pearls and the M&S dress I had bought for her. She had been very bright and alert all day, so much so that she got me to one side and said, 'Your aunty Jean's had two pieces of cake,' and later after a quick recce of who was supping what, said, 'Mind this lot don't drink all the wine; I want to make sure there's some left for the staff.'

Shortly after this my mother began to sharply decline. Not long after, I received the call to say I had to go back for the last time.

*

I sped back from London and sat next to Mum and took her hand. She was in and out of consciousness but she knew that I was there. I told her what a great childhood I had had. Knowing that she had heard this gave me some peace. I settled in next to her bed as visitors and nurses came and went.

The nurses had warned me that once someone is in decline in the way my mother was, they might start seeing people in the room who weren't there. It brought me straight back to my dad shouting, 'Mam!' in the bed just before he died and I assured them that I was prepared for it.

The days passed and I kept my vigil, chatting to my mum, trying to make sure she was as comfortable as possible. She looked so old and frail. The fact that she wasn't sitting up, immaculately dressed wearing her red lipstick, was still a bit of a shock to me. In fact, it was only a few weeks earlier that Mum had stopped reaching for her red lipstick and I knew then that she had given up. It makes me sad to think of that now. The nurses were wonderful, coming in to make sure I understood when anything was happening why it was happening. They encouraged me to talk to her, reminding me that hearing is one of the last things to go. I found real comfort in this and tried to talk to my mum as much as possible.

As my mother lay in her bed for what would be her final night, her arms, by now tiny and bony, began reaching up in the air. I sat next to her, watching in fascination. One would reach up and she would make a little noise, then it would go down, only for the other to be raised in the air, her fingers moving as if plucking the strings of a harp. On and on this went all night, reaching up relentlessly. I soon became worried that she may be exhausting herself but she seemed so compelled to continue, and it became quite eerily beautiful to watch.

The following day my mother had calmed down, her arms were no longer rising and falling. Joel had joined me at her bedside. She was slipping in and out of consciousness. The nurses changed shift and the new duty nurse came in to say hello to my mother.

'Hello, Margaret.'

My mother opened her eyes.

'You've got Susan and Joel.'

She suddenly became animated. 'Ah,' she said, 'Joel, my favourite person in the world.'

Joel and I looked at one another and laughed, nothing changes! My cousin Pauline arrived and a little later my aunty Jean and cousin Elizabeth came in to see Mum on their way back from a funeral and stayed for a while. When they left, David and Ali arrived. They had driven from Woking after calling me and being told that she was near the end. We were all gathered around the bed. Mum was very peaceful now, and her breathing had become faint and shallow.

At one point I got quite panicky thinking, 'I don't like this, I don't like the way her face is changing.' Her face seemed to be getting greyer, more lifeless, and I found this hard to watch. Then there was a moment that caught us all by surprise. I had taken my mother's top set of false teeth out but I had forgotten about the bottom set. Suddenly her lips puckered exaggeratedly then her mouth opened and all of a sudden these teeth shot out as if they had been delivered from the deep. We all laughed, shocked, but it was a moment of levity in this sad day. I knew that these were my mother's last hours but even so you are never truly prepared for it. And then she reached out, we helped her up, she sneezed, and then I felt the life leave her. As she lay back on the bed, her beautiful piercing blue eyes staring at me, I knew that she had gone.

Afterwards we all went outside and I got very upset, and one of the nurses came and asked if I'd like to go back in and see her. I wasn't sure that I did but I thought that I should, so I went back into the room. The nurses had dressed my mother and placed white roses across her breast. Her eyes were closed and she looked so peaceful.

It was such a kind thing for them to do and I was extremely grateful.

We had to wait for the undertakers to come and one of the nurses added another kindness. She brought in a box of wine, which was extremely gratefully received, and we all sat drinking it and talking. There felt like such a need to just talk and be together.

*

When I think back on the days after my mother's death it is always with a bit of bewilderment. There was so much to do in those following weeks that the actual activity somehow propelled me through. Unlike my father's funeral that took place within a matter of days of his death, my mum's had to be held a full two weeks afterwards. Susie was an absolute godsend. She is very organised and extremely good at planning things, so she stepped in and took me under her wing.

First of all we had to decide where the funeral would take place. There was the crematorium, or the crem, as we refer to it in the north. Mum was to be cremated but I always found ceremonies at the crem very perfunctory so I wanted a service elsewhere first. Next to the home where Mum had lived was a beautiful church so we called up and went to meet the vicar. He was fantastic, such a fun man. Susie and I suggested a few of Mum's favourite songs and he was very happy for us to have non-religious music, as well as hymns.

Whereas I would have made do with whatever was on offer, Susie wanted to make sure my mum had a right royal send off. She never sees obstacles anywhere; she just makes things happen. She looked around the church. 'We'll get a piano in,' she said, 'and I know the perfect vocalist.'

During the intervening two weeks between my mother dying and her funeral, I had to go back to the care home to clear out her belongings. Susie came with me. It was very sad and something I found extremely difficult. In her room there had been a picture of Mum and her sisters when they were younger. And there was a picture of Joel at his graduation, or so my mother thought. When my mum said that she would love a picture of him graduating, we didn't have the heart to tell her he hadn't gone to the ceremony. So we mocked up a picture of him with his mortarboard and certificate that was taken in my dining room! The other picture, which took pride of place, was a head shot of my German Shepherd, Brontë, which Joel had taken and Mum requested should be in her room. I might add that there were no pictures of me!

Brontë was our most beloved dog. When he was younger, Joel would stay at my parents when I was away working, but by the time he was sixteen he wanted to stay at home. I was worried about him in the house on his own so I decided that I would buy a guard dog.

We found Brontë and gave her that name because she was from Yorkshire. She immediately became part of the family. She dug everything up. Every plant, every flower was up and out of the ground as soon as my back was turned. Brontë lived to a ripe old age and she was thirteen when we had her put down. It was a very sad day for me, and more so because of how upset Joel was. Brontë was his dog and even though he was twenty-eight when she died he was inconsolable.

We never told my mother that Brontë had died. Nor did we tell her that we had another dog, Ebony, although I'm not sure why. I think she would have had something to say about me having another dog alongside Brontë. Ebony is a black Labrador and was my dog in *Jam and Jerusalem*. She was also with me on the set when I filmed *My Uncle Silas* and she was more at home in front of the camera than I was. Whenever my mother was around, before she went in the home, we'd pretend that Ebony was Susie's, as Susie lived next door to me. It became a ruse in which everyone seemed to be involved. Dean Sullivan used to thoroughly enjoy winding me up in front of my mum about Ebony. Ebony would be on the furniture and Dean would say to my mother, 'Look, Margaret, that dog. She's very badly behaved, isn't she?'

'Yes, she is,' my mother would agree. She loved Dean and would go along with everything he said.

'I tell you, Margaret, if that dog was Sue's it wouldn't behave like that, would it?' Susie would glare at Dean, trying not to laugh. He would continue, pretending not to notice, 'Susie, though, she lets that dog run riot.'

My mother would nod in agreement at the Gospel according to Dean while Susie and I would have our backs to him, trying to stop our shoulders betraying the fact that we were hysterical with laughter.

So Brontë had been my mother's firm favourite and it was sad to have to take those pictures away. I packed up her little amount of belongings and took them back to her house where there was the much larger task ahead of me. Something that has stayed with me about the process of clearing my mum's stuff was that in the end, what she really wanted with her were just a few photos containing her treasured memories. We spend so much of our lives buying and acquiring things but none of it seems to matter in those final months, certainly not in my mum's case: family was what had mattered.

When I set about tackling her house, Beryl and Peter, my mum's next-door neighbours, and my aunty Jean and Susie again were all fantastic; all on hand to help me as I trawled through Mum's belongings. We spent days sorting through them, some of the stuff she had kept for years. There were even wedding presents that were still in their box. I tried to throw away as much as I could but I am a hoarder and my mother's boxed wedding presents are now in my attic and no doubt will end up being passed on to Joel to either throw away or keep in his attic.

But what struck me most was the things of mine that she had kept that I had no idea she even had, programmes from theatre productions I'd been in, cuttings from papers and magazines of shows I'd appeared in. I was ever so touched. She would never in a million years have shared with me the fact that she was keeping these things.

*

The day of my mother's funeral finally arrived and we made our way to the church. The lovely thing about it taking place in the church next to the home was that some of the residents could attend, and as we pulled up outside they were all there waiting for her. I thought this was such a lovely thing, such a mark of respect for my mum. Then the staff all came into the service. I think my mother would have really loved this, as she had been so happy in her final months there.

Susie had had the order of service printed with two pictures of my mother on the front, one as a little girl and the other as an old lady, which was such a lovely personal touch. When my cousins entered the church carrying the coffin with the beautiful blue cloud of flowers on top, I just knew that we had done my mum proud. I read, as did Margot, and Dean said the eulogy which was very touching and funny.

'Nessun Dorma' was sung, as was 'Bring Him Home' from *Les Misérables*, and then as they carried the coffin out the recording of 'Do You Hear the People Sing?' again from *Les Misérables* was played. Everyone had the words in their song sheet and joined in. It is such a rousing emotional song and I was so pleased, it felt that we left on a high with a real celebration of my mother's life.

I had decided that only a few of us should attend the crematorium. I thought that it would be more bearable if it were just myself and Joel and my cousins who had carried the coffin. I wanted everyone else to leave the church after the ceremony and head straight to the wake. I wanted them to go out feeling it was a celebration and I suppose I wanted that last little time with my mother for myself and Joel. It was very sad to leave my mother but I found great comfort in her funeral and from the show of love from all the people who attended.

We had the wake at the golf club near my house in Warrington. We'd organised a great party. I was, of course, terribly sad but my mother had had a good life and a long life. There wasn't the same desperate sadness that I experienced at Veron's and Dom's funerals, it was the natural order of things. In the same way that we talk about a natural birth I feel that my mum had a natural death, which hadn't even involved medical intervention like my dad's.

*

I feel very strongly that those last few years with my mum saw a shift in the dynamic of our relationship. I had spent so many years trying to please my mother without ever feeling I had. But as she became weaker and more vulnerable she turned to me and it was having her need me that made me realise that we had a very strong bond. She was my mother and I loved her very much. In those final months and days in the home when she was frightened and needed someone there, it was me that she wanted, me whose hand she held. She looked at me with love and I was transported back to those times on her knee, waiting for *Listen With Mother*, feeling that the world began and ended with my family.

My mother and I had been through a lot over my lifetime, both together and separately, and there were times when I found her utterly exasperating. But she also gave me much to be proud of. She was a strong woman who provided me with a solid family bedrock on which to build my life. She may have struggled to let me go free, as the old proverb said, but she sure as anything gave me somewhere I could always return to.

Chapter Twenty-One

SINCE MY MOTHER died there have been a number of times when I have thought that I would really like her to share something that I know she would have loved. As I've mentioned, it is the everyday things that I miss the most – not being able to just call her up and tell her about a recipe I've read or something I'm watching on TV that I know she'd have enjoyed. Those small bits of life are the things I really miss sharing with my mother. However, there have also been a few big occasions where I wished both she and my dad were there.

In 2009 I was appointed OBE. It was 5 November. When I looked this up in my diary to check the exact date, the entry for the day says simply 9 a.m.: Palace, as if I am often at Buck House having tea with the Queen! I'm not. And this was to be a big honour.

I had actually met the Queen once before, about ten years previously, when she came to Liverpool. Paul McCartney was there and I hadn't seen him for years. It was the year of the Golden Jubilee and the Queen was visiting Liverpool and would re-open the Walker Art

Gallery. All the great and good of Liverpool had been assembled and my mother had bought a new outfit for the occasion. As we waited in line to be introduced to Her Majesty, someone said, 'And here's our own member of the Royle Family, Ma'am.'

To which she replied, 'Oh,' in a rather disapproving fashion.

I think I had thought the Queen might chat to my mother but she didn't and my mum was very disappointed. She didn't say it, but I could tell. A little later Paul McCartney made his way over and made a real fuss of my mother. She was over the moon. When he walked away my mother was beaming from ear to ear. *Not such a dirty Beatle now*, I thought!

*

In early autumn 2009, I had been standing in the kitchen with Joel who was visiting when I received a call from my agent. 'Hi, Sue, are you in? I'm sending something over.'

I needed some milk and the dogs were cross-legged. 'I have to pop out,' I said, 'but if I'm not here they can put it through the letterbox.'

I thought it was a script he was sending.

'You'll need to sign for this,' he assured me.

An hour later a courier arrived. I signed for my envelope and opened it to see ER stamped in large letters. I handed the pen back to the courier – he was a normal courier on a bike, not the liveried individual on horseback one might expect to be delivering something from the Palace – so the penny still hadn't dropped.

Joel looked over my shoulder. 'What's that?' he asked.

I read down the page. Slightly stunned, I announced, 'I've been awarded an OBE!'

The hardest thing was keeping it from everybody until the names were released to the press. Then the day itself arrived and I was allowed to take three guests, so I brought Joel, Margot and Susie. It was a strange experience going to Buckingham Palace. There's a familiarity to the place, having seen it a thousand times on TV and in passing. But stepping through the doors was like stepping into another world. The rooms are vast and seemingly endless. The walls are lined with paintings, the soldiers are very straight-backed. There is a real sense of history to the place but it is by no means a museum. It is a busy working palace. In fact, there were so many people going about their business that it felt like a small town.

The thing that struck me most was what a relaxed day it was. They are so obviously adept at putting on these events that everyone there made us feel at ease. We chatted to some of the accountants, who were very nice, and it dawned on me that for many of the people who worked there it was just that, a place of work.

An equerry came up to us. 'Excuse me,' he said. I looked at him, sure that we had stepped out of line somehow and were about to be told off. He dropped his voice: 'I'm not supposed to say this,' he quickly looked around to check that no one could see him transgressing any professional boundaries, 'but I'm a huge fan.' He smiled and walked off. I was delighted.

'Do you think the Queen watches *The Royle Family*?' Margot asked.

I thought about the Queen and Prince Philip and the gang sitting at Sandringham watching the Christmas special. 'Probably not,' I said.

'I bet the younger ones do, though,' Susie added. 'Prince Harry likes a laugh, doesn't he?'

I said my goodbyes to Joel, Margot and Susie, and another equerry took me through into a room where everyone else who was there to receive an award was gathered. We were divided into categories then put through our paces. I had a hook attached to my lapel so that the Queen could hook the medal on, no faffing with pins as I might have imagined.

'You will be called through,' the equerry told us, 'then as the person in front goes to receive their award you will take four steps forward.'

Four steps, I thought, *four steps*, sure I would forget all of this and collapse in a heap. I'm not a royalist but the sense of occasion and the surroundings made me quite nervous.

'Then when your name is read out,' he continued, 'the Queen is addressed as Your Majesty and then subsequently Ma'am, as in ham, not Ma'am as in farm.'

Mam not marm; *mam not marm*. Having spent years remembering long lines of dialogue I was sure all of this was going to leave my head the minute the equerry finished speaking.

'Then she will put her hand out to indicate that it is your time to leave. Take four steps backwards, never turning your back on Her Majesty.'

I was bamboozled. I decided to just follow what the person in front did and hope for the best.

I heard the Queen arrive and 'God Save the Queen' was played. We were to stay in another room until my name was called to go through. Eventually it was my time, and off I went, with a head full of four steps to the front, four steps to the right; mam, ham, spam. I stood waiting my turn, watching the Queen. For everyone in that room it was such a special occasion but I couldn't help thinking that for the poor Queen it must be like *Groundhog Day*. Doing the same thing over and over again.

Then someone read out, 'Sue Johnston, for services to charity and drama.'

And up I went, looking at the Beefeaters that lined the hall and thinking it was all very surreal.

I stood in front of the Queen; it felt very much like being called in front of the head teacher. I noticed that behind her was a chair upon which she'd placed her handbag. I thought this was a nice touch and made me think of my mother who always had her handbag nearby.

Although I don't think that Philip would have been as keen on fetching the bag for the Queen as my dad had been for my mum.

I approached her and stood before her. There was a moment of fumbling as she tried to hook the medal on to my lapel, which made us both smile, and then I stepped back.

The Queen looked at me quizzically as if trying to decide if she knew me. Then she said, 'It must be lovely to be able to combine drama and charity work.'

'Yes, Your Majesty, it is,' I said, thinking, *should I have said Ma'am*? 'Yes, it is lovely to combine drama and charity work.'

I had just repeated parrot fashion what she had said to me. What was I talking about? I wanted to say, 'Can I try that again? I must have a better line.' But then the arm shot out and I had to take my four steps backwards.

At the end of the ceremony the Queen came through the hall and nodded to everyone. I'm sure she was thinking, *Get me a gin and tonic.* In the paper next day it said, 'The Head of the Royal Family meets the Head of the Royle Family.'

I really missed my mum and dad that day. They were great traditionalists and for them to visit the Palace would have been a once-in-a-lifetime opportunity. And I know that I've said that my mother found it hard to say she was proud of me but she would have been as proud as a peacock that day.

*

The other and more important big occasion where I sorely missed my parents was Joel's wedding. Joel married his lovely wife Zoe in May 2010. Zoe and Joel had met at the Grapes pub in Manchester. The Grapes was co-owned by Liz Dawn and Zoe had worked there from the time she was at college. I always thought this was a great coincidence as Liz was a good friend of mine. Unlike me, Joel didn't know what he wanted to do when he left school, and it took a while to find his path, but by now he really found his passion as a professional photographer. Zoe was the icing on the cake.

I thought that the choosing of the outfit that I would wear would be fairly straightforward. I had checked with Zoe what the colour of the bridesmaid dresses was to be, and what colour her mother was wearing, and once I had this established I thought that the outfit would buy itself!

I was determined to look my best and do Joel proud without being over the top. I always remember the story of Raquel Welch, a mother so distraught that her son was getting married, so scared that this younger woman was going to usurp her in her son's affections, that she turned up at his wedding wearing a black dress. And not just any black dress; a buttock-skimming, cleavage-baring black dress. Imagine!

I found myself in Vivienne Westwood where I found a blue-spotted dress, it was wonderfully sculptured and would pull me in where necessary. The only problem was that it was sleeveless. When I was younger, if someone had asked me what I thought would be my greatest worry about my appearance when I got older, I would have thought a wrinkly face or saggy bottom. I wasn't to know that it would actually be my arms – that after the age of fifty-five I would never be able to wear a sleeveless top again, or not with any dignity. So if I was to buy this dress I would need a jacket. They had a perfect jacket to match but they only had it in a very small size. I thought about it for a moment and then just decided to buy it anyway. I would wear the jacket to the ceremony and get a cardigan to throw on in the evening. When I got home and tried on the outfit again I realised that the jacket was so tight that once my arms were in I wouldn't be able to raise them or lower them during the wedding. I tried to convince myself that this wasn't too much of a handicap. Why would I need to raise and lower my arms anyway? I thought, conning myself that a jacket I'd poured myself into would be fine.

The week before the wedding I was in Harvey Nichols in Manchester when I walked past the most perfect outfit. A muted silver-grey dress with a matching long coat from Calvin Klein. Suddenly my Vivienne Westwood seemed far too fussy, I had to have this instead. But then the sales assistant informed me that they didn't have it in my size. I was devastated. I might have chanced squeezing into a smaller jacket but not an entire outfit. In fear that

I might start sobbing, the sales assistant came to my rescue, locating the suit in my size back in London. I went down to pick it up – and while there I popped into Harrods and bought a matching hat and shoes in a matter of minutes.

The night before the wedding, Susie and I stayed with Joel, his best man and his ushers at Stanneylands Hotel near Wilmslow. We had dinner together and I made sure that the lads were all in bed at a reasonable hour.

The next morning we got up and headed to the Cheshire countryside. The venue was Sandhole Farm in Congleton, a converted barn overlooking a lake. The outhouses around the barn had been converted into cottages and we were to stay there that evening. It was such a beautiful setting. And unfussy, which really suited Joel and Zoe's laid-back attitude. Once there we felt cocooned, there was no traffic, it was such a tranquil place. It felt like the whole day would focus on Joel and Zoe, just as it should.

I headed to my room. From the window was a wonderful view of the Cheshire countryside and the lake. Once changed, a few of us gathered to have a glass of champagne and calm our nerves – I don't know what I had to be nervous about! When Joel came in I was swelled with pride. I had had a bespoke suit made for him and he looked so smart and handsome.

To have something handmade for him was something I really wanted to do and I know that my mother would be very pleased if she could have seen him. Well, I also know she would have asked how much it cost and on hearing the answer would have said, 'You can get a perfectly good suit in Marks without spending all that!' but she would have been secretly delighted that Joel was wearing a suit from Savile Row. I'm sure she'd have had a few choice words about me splashing out on Calvin Klein too!

We went through to the barn, the mood was very upbeat, everyone was in great spirits. I knew that Joel was so happy to be getting married to Zoe and we all felt the same for him. Once we entered the room where the ceremony would take place and I saw all those people gathered for them, I began to brim with tears and I had to concentrate on not crying. Seeing Beryl and Peter really touched me. Having spent so much time with my mum and dad when growing up, Joel had spent a lot of time with Beryl and Peter too. It was so lovely to see my family and friends all in one place for such a happy occasion and I beamed with pride.

We took our seats. Even though I knew that Zoe was in the building there is still that nervous expectation when waiting for the bride to arrive. The bridesmaids came first. Zoe had her sister Gemma, her two friends and Elizabeth, Margot's daughter. Elizabeth was beaming from ear to ear. Elizabeth is very special to us all and to have Zoe choose her for that day meant the world to Elizabeth. She had really enjoyed attending the dress fittings and getting to know the other brides-maids.

Zoe looked beautiful, like a Grecian goddess. Her dark hair fell loosely on her shoulders. As she walked towards Joel I realised she didn't have any flowers, which I thought must have been something she'd decided against, until I saw her sister running up the aisle later – she'd left them in her room by accident. Zoe's dad Kevin is Scottish and was wearing a kilt. In fact a few of the men were wearing kilts so there was quite a bit of leg on show!

One of the kilt wearers was Andy Hay. Andy had been asked to read as he had always been very close to Joel throughout his life. He chose a passage from *Romeo and Juliet* and he was very nervous as he wanted to make sure that whatever he chose and how he read was right for Joel. He had also prepared a song but he didn't perform it; instead he sat straight down after reading. I knew that he had planned to sing as I'd seen him tuning up his guitar. 'Where's the song?' I whispered.

'I thought I might bore everyone!' he whispered back.

But when it was time for the couple to sign the register, Joel invited Andy up to sing. He had made up his own version of a Scottish folk song, 'Marie's Wedding', and changed it to 'Zoe's Wedding'. He taught us all the words and we all sang with him. It was a perfect end to the ceremony, everyone singing along. I was so happy by then that I was mopping up the tears.

For me, all the worries and anxieties of being a single mother were washed away. I had often felt that Joel had missed out having a father in his life, being brought up by his mum. But I felt like I didn't need to worry any more.

Joel is also a very loved man; he is loyal to his friends and has found a wife with a 'proper family' that he has joined. There is Zoe and her sister Gemma and her husband Dave, and their mum and dad Lorraine and Kevin, and they have been exceptionally warm and welcoming to both Joel and me.

During his Father of the Bride speech Kevin took out a silver goblet. 'We have a tradition in Scotland,' he said pouring whisky into the goblet, 'we share a whisky in a Welcome Cup. We would like to welcome Joel, and in turn Sue, into the McFarlane family.'

He came around and offered me a drink, I took it and drank. I was extremely touched by this gesture, even though I'm not overly keen on whisky!

Veron's daughter Gemma was there too. It was lovely to see her with her husband Alex, who she had married the year before. I felt like my family was all grown up. It was such a magical day and my resounding memory is of a sea of happy faces; I couldn't have wished for more for my son.

The evening do was fabulous and we all kicked back, eating, dancing and being very merry indeed! And I can say unequivocally that Joel's wedding day was the happiest and proudest day of my life.

Epilogue

SITTING AND THINKING about my life has made me realise that, although there have been many ups and downs along the way, I have had a very happy and fulfilled one so far. I was privileged to have my parents with me for as long as they were, and I am very lucky to have Joel and the loving and close relationship I share with him.

I haven't had an actual relationship myself for quite some time but I can honestly say I don't miss it! I spent so much of my early life thinking that I had to be part of a couple for my life to have meaning. But now I am single and happily alone I realise that there really is more to life than worrying if a man is going to call when he says he will. That's not to say I'm writing men off altogether, I just don't feel being part of a couple is something I need to define me.

Careerwise, I find myself at another one of those 'jumping off' points in my life where I'm not sure what I'll be doing next. *Waking the Dead* has finished and I'm excited and a little nervous at the prospect of embarking on something new, but I've done it before and I'll do it again. It might be theatre, it might be TV or film, but whatever it is it won't be dull. And as long as people are willing to have me in their living rooms I'll keep on acting. Oh, and as long as I can still learn the lines!

I look back at my life so far and I'm thankful for my friends and family because without them to fall back on I'm not sure I would always have been so ready to take my numerous leaps of faith.

Reading over the earlier chapters of this book I can now see that I really must have given my parents sleepless nights as they tried to get their grammar-educated daughter to stay in a good stable job to no avail. I sometimes think I find it hard to make decisions but I was very single-minded in my desire to be an actress. I pursued it as a career, I didn't just fall into it and hope for the best. And I am very grateful that I did because I have been given the most amazing opportunities and been allowed to play a number of great characters who people have genuinely taken to their hearts.

And so, dear reader, the end of this part of my story is nigh. From beginning writing this book, to penning these final words, I feel like I've come on that much over-used term these days: a journey. I began by thinking that my relationship with my mother was difficult and have ended by feeling very much loved and looked after by her, even though she wasn't good at showing it.

From thinking about how she cared for me when I was younger, to remembering how I felt when I discovered she had kept mementos of mine from over the years, I have come to the conclusion that my mum was my mum. She didn't do the things the way that I would have liked her to a lot of the time, but she did them her way. And everything she ever did had her family at the heart of it. I did keep parts of my life from her but that was just our relationship and I have accepted that. It didn't mean I was lying to her; I was just keeping her happy in the world that she had fought so hard to build around her. She didn't like change and I did. *Vive la différence*!

*

And as I sit here, coughing from a bad chest I'm just shaking off, wearing red lipstick and eating my lunch from Marks', something has just occurred to me...I think I'm turning into my mother!

June 2011

Acknowledgements

With thanks to my dear friends and family, they mean everything. They know who they are. To Anne-Marie, my editor, who got me. And to Liverpool Football Club, my passion, in the hope this will buy me free tickets to away games!